Praise for Denise Conde and
The Valor of Generation X

Wow! What a refreshing look at imperative information every person can benefit from. This book is a clever play on music from Gen X artists. [In this way, Denise] helps braid together a culture of people, along with their music.

This book will be impactful to many generations, as they all need to be understood. The elegant writing has a way of allowing people to feel smart and included. As Denise asks questions, it feels like you are in a dialogue with her, and she makes you feel calm, capable, and empowered.

As a trauma specialist, I travel the world teaching people about how to "stay in the body." Specifically, I teach them about the importance of knowing how to regulate their nervous system. In this book, Denise does a fantastic job of explaining some of the most complicated concepts that I teach, and she makes it all so easy to understand.

This book will certainly be one of the first books each of my patients reads as they begin their own growth journey.

Thank you to Denise for sharing her story and being so vulnerable. This is never an easy charge, but when you're called to this work and you know that you have a story to share, it can be so rewarding.

I hope this book helps many people to find their courage and locate a safe space to share their story.

Trauma Specialist and Founder and CEO of
Bridging Harts Psychotherapy and Training Institute

We all have issues we're working through, whether it's a recent emotional event that has left us reeling or a deep, traumatic wound from childhood. I healed from breast cancer holistically six years ago, so I know how difficult it is to work through serious issues and trauma alone.

Denise approaches everything from her heart and soul, offering endless amounts of patience, love, and understanding. I wish I had had the benefit of her support and guidance when I was working through my trauma. It would've made a world of difference!

—ANDREA ZACCARELLA
Certified Holistic Health Coach, Certified Holistic Cancer
Coach, and Active Health Group Member

The VALOR

of Generation X

HOW THE COURAGEOUS ARE FINDING
A NEW PATH TO GROWTH AND LOVE

DENISE CONDE

NYX PUBLISHING

First published in 2025 by Onyx Publishing, an imprint of Notebook Group Limited, Arden House, Deepdale Business Park, Bakewell, Derbyshire, DE45 1GT.

www.onyxpublishing.com

ISBN: 9781913206741

A CIP catalogue record for this book is available from the British Library.

Typeset by Onyx Publishing of Notebook Group Limited.

To my husband, Michael, and my daughters, Grace and Maggie.

Contents

Disclaimer

The stories in this book are based on the author's personal experiences and their perception of their personal memories. This information is accurate to the best of the author's knowledge. The author has purposefully left out the names of some, in the interest of protecting their anonymity.

Preface

With every healing journey in life, there inevitably comes the dark night of the soul. This is when you begin to truly see the parts of yourself that you have previously denied or been unconscious of.

The dark night of the soul usually occurs after something horrible has happened in your life. For me, it happened when I was reading a book called *Out of the Fog: Moving From Confusion to Clarity After Narcissistic Abuse* by Dana Morningstar. I was looking for guidance on how to piece my life back together after a terribly catastrophic event, orchestrated by my mother, that had happened in my life. It was when I got to the section about healthy relationships versus unhealthy relationships that realization struck. Suddenly, with vivid clarity, I could identify the parts of myself, as a partner and a parent, that I wasn't so proud of. I couldn't believe what I now saw in myself.

I began crying tears of mortification. I wanted to die. I physically tossed the book from where I was in bed, curled into a fetal position, and grabbed my blanket and threw it over my head. How had I *become* this person?

My sobs were relentless. I felt as though I was shrouded in darkness from which I would never escape; as though there was no way to climb out to the light.

Now, I *am* the light, and I guide others to the light they hold within.

Every hero's journey starts like this—with some sort of formative moment—and the universe will keep flipping your world upside down until the lesson it's sending your way is learned and you pursue the path that is true to your heart and authentically yours. It will keep knocking on the door to your unconscious to awaken you, and the knock will keep getting louder until you finally open the door to transcend into enlightenment; until you open the door into your valor.

Introduction

This book is written for those of you who were born into Generation X (somewhere around 1965–1980).

Google anything about our generation, and you will see that we are known as the "middle child," or the "forgotten generation" — the population that came between the baby boomers and the millennials. Yet there are approximately *sixty-five million* of us.

We were the kids who had all the independence. We were left to our own devices, to survive on our own from sunup to sundown while our parents worked (if one of your parents was home during the day, you were one of the lucky ones). We roamed the neighborhoods, riding our bikes for miles, drinking from garden hoses, and packing our own lunches (or eating on the fly), wholly unsupervised by adults. Our signal to come home was the streetlights coming on or the sun going down.

We were the youth gone wild.

Our older siblings were responsible for us, and they parented us (or we parented our younger siblings). We fought our own battles among the neighborhood kids and the kids at school. We invented a system of social justice that we proudly built and abided by.

In contrast to our street life, we were expected to conform to the rules at school, or we'd be "disciplined" at home.

While all this freedom made us very independent, resilient, gritty, and determined (with a very keen work ethic), it also left many of us very alone, neglected, and abused. A lot of Gen Xers had highly stressed parents and dysfunctional homes, yet we still think of our upbringings as "normal," at least "for the time." This was just the way it was, after all. It *was* our normal.

Most of our parents were from the baby boomer generation — the generation that fought in Vietnam and realized the American dream. They did this after *their* parents (and parents' parents) migrated to the US during World War II, and after all those before them survived the Great Depression.

Is this a history lesson? Well, kind of. It's important for us to look at our parents, grandparents, great-grandparents, and so on, and consider what they survived during their lifetimes. By doing so, we learn not only from the history of the world, but also from the history of the country and family we were each born into. While all that our ancestors accomplished should be celebrated, there is currently an undeniable mental health crisis that is happening worldwide, and this can be traced back to these older generations. This begs the question of, when will we begin to heal and lean into our valor?

"Valor" is a word that is often associated with great courage in the face of danger, especially in battle, and at one point in my life, I felt as though my day-to-day existence was a constant battle. I was facing problems *everywhere*: in my marriage; in my relationship with my daughters; with my ex; with my parents; with my sisters... everyone. I was very unhappy, I repeated many patterns, and I constantly swore I would make changes in my marriage and in my relationship with my kids, only to start the same cycle all over again, time after time. Around and around I'd go, stuck in the same pattern, aware of how deeply unhappy I was inside and yet feeling powerless to change it.

On a beautiful warm spring day that I will never forget, my husband pulled his chair close to mine, looked me in the eyes, and said, "If something doesn't change with you, I can't do this anymore. I do not feel loved by you, and something has changed in you since your father died. I need you to make some changes, and if you don't... well, I just can't do this anymore."

I felt like something inside me had caved in on itself, because I knew he was right. Still, I couldn't put my finger on where and how things had gone so wrong.

I thought deeper.

I was no longer grieving my father's death—it had been four years since his passing—but I was still in a deep, dark place in my soul. I wasn't giving my husband, myself, or my daughters the love they deserved. I didn't even really understand what loving yourself *meant*. If asked, I always would have said that I loved myself, but I knew that wasn't true.

I was desperate to make changes, but didn't know how to. This was my second marriage, and it was about to fall apart.

I had forgiven my father and mother for the abuse that I'd endured at their hands, but here I was, still frozen in the past and in my outdated trauma responses, stuck like an iceberg that had been in the same storm in the same spot in the arctic for centuries. I felt misunderstood, unheard, unappreciated, unseen, and unloved.

To make matters even more confusing, my marriage wasn't all that was falling apart in my life; my career choice was up in the air, too. I'd spent twenty years as a special education teacher, and as comfortable as I had become with this career, and as great as retirement (with all its benefits and a mere six years away) was looking, I knew I was being called to do something else with my life.

It turned out this calling was to help my fellow Gen Xers navigate their way to not only loving themselves, but also becoming their own leaders in life (and realizing their valor).

Newly determined (and with the motivation of my husband's ultimatum), I set out on a path of true self-reflection and healing. I also suggested that my immediate family embark on this journey. I was determined to break their cycles of generational trauma.

My husband and daughters are my "why." They are why I started this journey. In addition to them, *you* are my "why!"

Before we dive in, I want you to take a moment to intentionally ask yourself, *What is my "why?"* Why are you reading this book? What do you wish to gain from it? Maybe it's a stronger relationship with yourself, your kids, or your partner. Maybe it's more peace, clarity, or love (for yourself and others). Whatever your intention, I'm confident we can get there together.

Throughout this book, we will investigate how trauma affects the nervous system and our ability to heal. I'll offer helpful suggestions on where to begin with this.

We will also dive into the subconscious and how you can examine yours. This is important: the subconscious greatly influences how you behave with your partner and your kids, as well as how you feel about yourself. Gen Xers tend to have a ton of patterns of behavior that need to be unearthed if they are to deepen their exploration of the subconscious, so in that chapter, we will spend a lot of time exploring the conditioned role you might be playing within your family of origin and your partnerships.

This leads into the next chapter of family enmeshment and hierarchical issues. This topic is, I find, rarely discussed, even though it has a huge impact on the self. Family enmeshment and hierarchical issues tend to manifest as self-betrayal and emotional distance within our most intimate relationships.

Narcissism is a hot topic these days, and we will also cover this topic in this book. I will share my personal experiences with narcissism, and I will also share how you can identify narcissistic traits within others and yourself (and what to do about them). Here's a hint: boundaries are key.

Next, we will discuss marriage and partnership at length—because we all deserve love! *Unconditional* love. Maybe that idea—that everyone deserves love—is something you currently reject, or maybe you're unclear on what unconditional love truly means and looks like. Many of us learned what love "should" look like based on how we were raised. This chapter will give you clarity on the differences between a healthy relationship and one that may need some work. I'll also be offering tools and suggestions on how to improve your intimate relationships.

Parenting from the subconscious, the impact of divorce on our kids, coparenting, and parent alienation are all (intertwined) topics that are near and dear to my heart. These topics are practically never raised in "mainstream" discourse, and they need to be brought to the light. Conscious parenting requires releasing the ego and any "hierarchy conditioning" that is telling you that your children are somehow "less than" you and that you are the much more superior and all-knowing being. If that statement rubbed you the wrong way, these chapters are for you. There's always time to shift your parenting paradigm, even if your children are now adults.

Finally, we need to heal ourselves from the mind, body, and spirit, so this will be the topic of the final chapters of this book. These things are not separate from one another. My courses are riddled with proof of this, and science is currently catching up to spirituality in that sense. So, we will be taking a similarly holistic approach in this book. I was once a naysayer when it came to certain religious practices—many of us have been manipulated, controlled, and fearmongered through religious beliefs and teachings—but I will lead you down a spiritual path that serves me and is relevant to today's societal landscape. Even if you currently reject any type of spirituality, this could be game changing for you.

Speaking of my courses (and just to give you the reassurance that you have come to the right place!), this is what my clients have to say about me and my results-driven courses:

Thank you for walking through this journey with me. Your inspirational words make me want [to heal] even more. You are a very smart, loving, and caring woman. I'm lucky to have you as a friend. You've opened my eyes to a new world. I'm forever grateful!

—DAWN M.

Thank you, Denise! I appreciate you and your work more than you know.

—JENNIFER B.

Your course did a great job of both laying foundational work for those that may be unfamiliar with any of these methods and for offering extension opportunities, to deepen learning and practice for those that do have background knowledge. The activities were appropriate and eye-opening. Thank you for helping to support my own personal growth.

—NICOLE P.

Denise is definitely one cool guide! She has helped me learn a lot about myself, and after reading this, I will have to do some more work. I am forever a work in progress.

—KATE W.

Denise Conde has provided an excellent, easy to understand program to help heal the mind and soul. Whether you were the family scapegoat or not, Denise's teachings on narcissism and restoration provide helpful and excellent social knowledge everyone can benefit from. I loved how practical, personal, and experiential the teachings delivered by Denise were.

—MELANIE S.

I'm honored to have received, and am so grateful for, these testimonials. This book is like a "cliff note" version of my courses. It will guide you through the process of self-love and -awareness, in mind of your life and upbringing as a Gen Xer. Only when you begin to do the work and become self-aware will you be able to make significant life changes that not only affect you, but also those around you (and the generations to come). That's powerful shit, and you, my friend, are one powerful Generation Xer!

Before we begin, I strongly suggest that if you have the paper version of this book, you interact with it. Mark the pages with Post-Its, underline or highlight, write notes directly on the pages, reread it (whether from cover to cover or just specific sections that resonated with you)... After all, this book is for you and no one else! This is your valor we're talking about here, and a small act of self-love and a gift you can give to yourself is the permission to interact with this book. So, draw all over it!

One more suggestion: music has always been extremely therapeutic for me, as it has been for most of my fellow Gen Xers, so I've included the names of songs that are greatly loved by Gen Xers everywhere throughout this book. I encourage you to listen to these songs as and when they come up, to deepen the meaning behind each section.

Okay, let's dive in!

1

Comfortably Numb:
Resurrect the Nervous System

L ISTEN TO THE SONG *Comfortably Numb* by Pink Floyd before or during the reading of this chapter, to set the mood and tone.

When I reached that point in my life where I found myself experiencing problems in every single one of my relationships, I dismissed the idea that my childhood may be the reason for the issues I was facing. In fact, I avoided speaking about my childhood abuse at all, and actually continued to be subjected to this same abuse (unknowingly) until the day I finally chose me, at the age of forty-seven. Up until that point, it had all just become so normalized in my life that the idea of putting myself first felt selfish.

I wasn't aware of the imprint these years of abuse had left on my soul. Besides, the past had passed, so why would I want to dig up those old traumatic memories again? I'd gone to counseling sessions in my early thirties while I'd been suffering with depression and didn't want to do it again. (This is a common theme among many of us Gen Xers.) I also didn't want to be vulnerable and to talk about the many horrible things *I* had done in my past.

The ego likes to protect you and keep you exactly where you are— somewhere that feels safe, familiar, and comfortably numb—but I needed to get uncomfortable. I needed to get as close as possible to the little girl I once was and the woman I was meant to be, so I could truly understand myself.

The truth was, I struggled to trust anyone with my heart and my truth. I'd experienced physical and emotional abuse, neglect, abandonment, family enmeshment, narcissistic abuse, scapegoating, and more, all at the hands of the very people who were supposed to love and protect me.

I wasn't the only one. Many Gen Xers I know were hit, yelled at, and told they deserved their beating during their childhoods. Even today, this is still normalized or dismissed as something that was acceptable or appropriate "for the time." Us Gen Xers often joke about the "weapon of choice" our parents would use on us when we were children, whether a belt, wooden spoon, hand, hairbrush, or whatever was available at that moment. Let's not forget the silent treatment being used as a weapon, too!

This was the way parents disciplined at that time (and it was widely accepted). My belief once I entered adulthood was that I had "gotten over it." I'd moved on. I'd forgiven my parents and continued my relationship with them as an adult, as most of us do. After all, they didn't hit me anymore. Yet the fear and threat I used to feel around them during those all-important childhood years unconsciously remained in my body into adulthood, which often made family gatherings very difficult. I usually couldn't wait until the gathering ended, so preoccupied with my stream of agitated thoughts during the event that I struggled to enjoy the moment.

These feelings of "fight-or-flight" were difficult for me to reconcile with the people in front of me. After all, my parents had beautiful parts to them. They could be loving, fun, and caring. This is what often makes it so difficult to speak of the abuse you once endured at the hands of your parents, or to even define or think of it as abuse. A child's natural desire is to love their parents and to take all the love that comes their way (even if the love is conditional and entrenched in a wider context of abuse). In my case specifically, my parents had many friends and were well-liked within the community. People still come up to me today and tell me how much they used to love my mother and father. They did many wonderful things for others. Still, I was traumatized by the not-so-shiny sides of my parents' personalities.

It's no coincidence that throughout my childhood, I always found myself surrounded by friends who were experiencing a similar type of abuse. One of my friends pointed out to me at the age of forty that she and I (along with several of the other girls we hung out with in high school) had had fathers who were violent alcoholics. I had never realized this before. When I became an adult, almost every other teacher I worked with also had violent or alcoholic parents. My friendships and coworker bonds had been forged through trauma, unbeknownst to me. I had become "comfortably numb."

Everything I have described here can be traced back to one thing…

The Nervous System

Most people are not aware of the impact that abuse (of any sort) has on the wiring of the brain and the nervous system. If, for example, you were raised in a home with emotionally immature parents who argued regularly (and refused to admit that their fighting had an impact on you), this will have had a huge effect on you, neurologically and biologically.

Some common childhood experiences you might have had as a Gen Xer are:

- Being at the brunt of fights or complete silence, leaving everyone else walking on eggshells.
- Being yelled at or ignored for not making the choices your parents would have made.
- Being called names.
- Being abandoned by an alcoholic parent(s).
- Being ruled with manipulation and burdened with shame and guilt.
- Being subjected to hyper-religious beliefs (e.g., being told you will burn in hell for your actions or that you would "pay for your sins").
- Being blamed for your parents' emotional dysregulation (e.g., for "making them mad").
- Being made your parents' confidant about the problems in their marriage or the problems they were facing with their other children (i.e., your siblings).
- Being made your parents' "caregiver" or "protector," rather than them caring for and protecting *you*, as their child.

All these events have an impact on the nervous system. This is why I am starting with the topic of the nervous system: the tremendous impact that remains in the body years (and even decades) after the event or behavior has ended is often too large to comprehend. The brain and body remembers everything it experienced, and this memory often manifests as anxiety, depression, self-hatred, addictions, diseases, and more.

If you look at the word "disease" and dissect it, it can be read as "dis-ease." Hopefully that helps you to better understand what I'm getting at here! The nervous system is at dis-ease (i.e., "not at ease," i.e., no longer in homeostasis, i.e., no longer regulated) when it has been subjected to trauma, which makes the individual in question feel hypervigilant and unsafe in their own body. They are always on high alert, and this means their brain interprets neutral "outside" information as a possible threat. You may know this as being in "fight-or-flight." For me personally, this took the form of fits of rage, overdrinking, anxiety, depression, and terrifying childhood nightmares (and then new ones that emerged in adulthood).

Does this sound familiar?

I took antidepressants after having my second daughter, but these made my symptoms either worse or no better, which is often the case for many.

My point? Abuse is not something you just "get over." The body — specifically, the nervous system — *remembers*. As explained by Bessel van der Kolk in *The Body Keeps the Score* (which has been an incredibly inspiring and influential body of work guiding my own development and transformation):

> We now know that trauma compromises the brain area that communicates the physical, embodied feeling of being alive. These changes explain why traumatized individuals become hypervigilant to a threat at the expense of spontaneously engaging in their day to day lives. They also help us understand why traumatized people often keep repeating the same problems and have such trouble learning from their experience. We now know that their behaviors are not the result of moral failings or signs of lack

of willpower or bad character—they are caused by actual changes in the brain.[1]

Before we go on, let's discuss the wiring of the brain and nervous system through a simple analogy. (I like simple. Don't you?) Imagine the wiring inside the brain as a whole bunch of wires that are connected. Some wires are thicker than others, and some are thin. All branch out into the body in the form of nerves down your neck, spine, arms, legs, and toes.

When you were a child, all your wires were thin, baby wires, and as you aged, some wires became thicker. This means that when you were a kid, your wires were pliable and easily bent, but as you aged, they became thicker and not so easy to bend.

Say that as a child, you were yelled at. This fired the wires in your brain that told you to be on high alert, and, consequently, you learned to not do the thing that you got yelled at for. That wire, for a short time, held onto the memory of the feeling that you felt when you were being yelled at (such as alarmed, startled, or scared). In other words, your body stored and remembered this feeling, and this temporarily knocked your nervous system out of homeostasis (the neutral state of calm). After some time passed, you went back to being calm—your body returned to homeostasis—and you moved on.

Let's then say that you were *repeatedly* yelled at throughout the day and week, or often heard others in your home yelling. In *this* situation, your body didn't have the time to recover and return to homeostasis, so it remembered this feeling *and* your body's alarm system stayed on high alert for danger, not temporarily, but permanently. Suddenly, you could no longer turn off your alarm system. Instead, you started being subjected to what felt like a constant stream of violent attacks on your body.

---

[1] van der Kolk, B. (2014): *The Body Keeps the Score*. Viking Books (p. 3).

When this happens, your "wires" thicken, getting bigger and bigger as they store this overwhelming feeling in your body.

As your wires get "clogged up" with more and more trauma responses, there is an apparent change in your personality, and this is often excused away as "a phase you're going through." Perhaps you suddenly develop signs of anger, anxiety, depression, stomach issues, ADD or ADHD, anorexia, bulimia, or social issues among peers. Perhaps you begin using drugs or alcohol (or some other coping mechanism) to self-soothe, not knowing that this is just your body's way of attempting to get some sense of control so it can return to homeostasis and (relative) calm.

I can hear the peanut gallery in the background already: "All this comes from *yelling*? Bullshit!" Remember, your ego is a tricky beast and will try to keep you safe and comfortable, and that sometimes means preventing you from opening your mind up to new information. If you are to grow and learn, you need to get uncomfortable.

Our takeaway here is that *the nervous system remembers*. It remembers *all* significant or repeated memories. All those wires hold the feeling that was caused when you were initially yelled at as a child, and if you were *repeatedly* yelled at, your body never returned to homeostasis at all.

This situation becomes even more complicated when you realize that people often yell in the first place because *they* have a dysregulated nervous system out of their own fear or anxiety, too (thereby creating generational cycles when trauma is left unhealed).

Let's say that the child in our example gets a counselor and is put on medication, and there seems to be temporary relief for the child and the parents. The medication has successfully turned off or dulled the alarms going off in the child's body. The child now doesn't feel depressed or anxious (or whatever the symptom was), at the price of feeling numb or "not inside their own body" or "not like themselves" all the time.

This is not a long-term happy ending. Research shows that medication should not be the only source of nervous system regulation, because the nervous system is built to regulate the body and keep it in homeostasis; to keep you feeling what's going inside your body. So, it's not good to be medically "numbed" all the time. When you numb the sensations inside your body exogenously, the nervous system can stay stuck in one of the four triggered nervous system states ("fight," "flight," "freeze," or "fawn") as it tries to process and realign to calm.

Many people do need medication as a short-term solution to give them an initial "boost" when their wires have thickened into adulthood. When a dysregulated nervous system has been left untreated and the wires have become harder to bend and "clogged up," the wires can no longer receive new information. In other words, those with a dysregulated nervous system can remain stuck in "survival mode," or "fight-flight-freeze-fawn," where nearly everything feels like an attack on the body. Such people view all new information as a threat and are constantly triggered and hypervigilant, even in moments of relative "calm" or "safety." In such a scenario, medication can offer some quick "wins." Still, medication alone won't heal the root cause of the problem.

Why have I used the specific example of yelling to illustrate what happens to the nervous system when it is exposed to stressful or triggering situations? Because I feel that you will be able to recall that feeling that courses through your body when you're yelled at. *Now* think of what must happen to the nervous system when it is exposed to war, violence, rage, radical religious beliefs, sexual assault, narcissistic abuse, repeated mental and psychological abuse, and so on. All this terror is stored in the wires inside the victim's body, and suddenly, the body is at "dis-ease," creating a breeding ground for illness.

Here's where the ego wants to start making a comparison: "Well, I was never at war as a kid. I wasn't even hit, *and* my parents didn't yell. That must mean my nervous system is good and better than those who have experienced the things that I never have. My ego and I are going to leave this conversation now, because this doesn't apply to us."

I understand why this is a common reaction to this conversation, but I'd like to direct your attention to the fact that when love for a child is withheld or is used as a parent's manipulation tactic, or when the child is ignored, neglected (physically or emotionally), abandoned, shamed, guilt-tripped, reality-denied, overtalked, prevented from expressing themselves freely, overly criticized, held responsible for the dysregulation of a parent's nervous system, assigned as the caretaker for an ill parent or their siblings at an early age, blamed for all the family's problems (i.e., made a scapegoat), or told that being the "perfect golden child" is where they get their value from, the nervous system reacts in the same way as it does to war, violence, abuse, and so on.

Does that feel like a lot to unpack? If so, don't worry. You're not alone in those overwhelming feelings.

The truth is, it's not all about violence and rage and yelling. Those things, for me, were the obvious signs of nervous system dysregulation. The *not*-so-obvious, confusing, and often-overlooked causes of nervous system dysregulation are the things that form a steady stream of underlying conflict and chaos in the home. And the stream is usually very steady indeed: if there *isn't* conflict or a problem in a household, someone who already has a dysregulated nervous system will often look to *create* a conflict or a problem. Like a drug addict needing a hit, the brain and nervous system, strangely, crave continued dysregulation, and this usually culminates in good old drama.

Moments of calm and peace feel boring for a dysregulated nervous system. In fact, these moments can feel deeply unsettling when you're used to constant chaos and clamor. This is because the dysregulated body adapts to feel more alive when it's *out* of homeostasis — that is, when it's *not* calm and at peace — *especially* as the wires thicken with age.

You can watch this unfold in real time on social media. People who are addicted to conflict often attempt to bring others into arguments by judging them, name-calling, forcing their views and opinions onto them, and saying rude, hurtful, and disrespectful things.

The silent onlookers who don't involve themselves in these conflicts directly but are addicted to watching them unfold are also looking for the same "hit," only this behavior gives a false sense of superiority: "I'm not involved, so I'm better than the ones involved in the conflict." I know I've been involved in both scenarios!

Coping Mechanisms: How Not to Regulate the Nervous System

Alcohol by the Barenaked Ladies is a great song to listen to when we're talking about how not to regulate the nervous system. Give it a listen and focus on the part about self-control and self-abuse.

So many of us have addictions, and these beautiful people are often treated as though they have a disease. However, most substance abusers *become* substance abusers simply because they are using the substance in question as a "coping mechanism" for their dysregulated nervous system. I was once a prime example of such a person.

Substances are, of course, not the only means of coping with a dysregulated nervous system. Coping can take many forms, such as bulimia, anorexia, overeating, cutting, hair-pulling, skin-picking, overspending (retail therapy), gambling, sex addiction, overworking, perfectionism, "doom-scrolling," binge-watching, hoarding... the list goes on and on. The common denominator is, the chosen coping mechanism(s) becomes the favored way in which the sufferer can feel good, alive, and in control, and the person is usually unaware that this behavior even *is* a coping mechanism. They normalize it.

I quickly got into the rut of looking forward to the end of a workday or weekend solely so I could grab a drink. I quite literally planned around my drinking. I thought this constant craving for a drink was a normal reaction to a jam-packed, often-stressful life, but really, it was an attempt to regulate, or "numb," my nervous system.

How to Regulate the Nervous System

Of course, the nervous system is complex, and any oversimplification here has been made for the purpose of ensuring you, my reader, can get to grips with the underlying principles of how it works. More specifically, I want you to understand a) how feelings and events are stored in the body and b) the fact that the brain and the nervous system, miraculously, can be *rewired* in such a way that will allow you to make the changes in life that you want to.

I distinctly remember feeling disgusted when I read about the wiring in the brain and body. You're telling me that all I endured from childhood and adulthood is *stuck inside my body*? I couldn't wrap my head around it. I was pretty pissed, and I didn't believe for a second that I held the power to rewire my brain and nervous system. Instead, I wanted instant results from conventional sources. I wanted to call a surgeon and beg them to fix me.

My attitude and beliefs now couldn't be more different.

Trust me when I say that rewiring your own brain for a brighter future *is* possible. I did it (despite all my trepidation)! Sure, you might be dealing with some pretty thick wires, but they are still just wires. Can wires of all sizes be bent into new shapes and sizes, with the right tools? Yep! Which is fabulous news, isn't it?

The facts are, you were gifted with the power to reshape your future. You have everything you need inside your amazing body to do so. Here are some activities that regulate the nervous system (in no particular order, as everyone is different):

- Journaling.
- Breathwork.
- Yoga.
- Meditation.
- Going on walks out in nature while taking in your surroundings.
- Getting out in the sun.
- Sitting by moving water.
- Grounding yourself to the earth by taking your shoes off and walking on the grass.
- Hugging a tree.
- Gardening.
- Cold therapy (i.e., slowly introducing yourself to thirty seconds of a lukewarm shower and then making it colder for longer periods, or immersing your face or hands in a bowl of cold water).
- Having Epsom salt baths.
- Laying in the snow and making a snow angel.
- Getting a massage.
- Hugging for more than ten seconds.
- Singing along to a song.
- Stretching.
- Staring at the moon.
- Going on a bike ride.
- Watching the sun go down.
- Dancing.
- Sitting by a campfire.
- Skiing.

- Watching nature.
- Wrapping yourself in a weighted blanket.
- Tapping.
- Engaging in reiki therapy.
- Going to the theater.
- Acting.
- Drawing.
- Painting.
- Playing an instrument.
- Listening to different sound frequencies (there are so many free recordings on YouTube).
- Doing sound bowl meditations.

...and so on!

As a fun little hack: your nervous system is going to respond more effectively to the things it really enjoys, especially if it's something you enjoyed doing as a kid. Don't be afraid to try something new too, though.

Sounds too easy, doesn't it? Just go for a walk and all your problems will be solved. Well... not exactly. As you may have guessed, this is just one piece of the puzzle (but it's a big piece).

Why do these practices assist in regulating the nervous system? The easiest explanation is, they bring your nervous system to the present moment, rather than to the past or future. When you allow yourself to be present in the moment (whether that's in the form of watching the sun go down in all its beautiful glory, having a soothing massage, singing a song at the top of your lungs, or dancing), you are living in the moment and nowhere else. This signals to the body that you are safe and in a pleasurable, joyful state, thereby calming and soothing any alarms going off.

The more regularly you do these things, the more you will stay present and regulated. The catch is, this is something *you* need to do, and no one else. No one is coming to save you (though do reach out for help, if needed).

Keep dancing and singing the songs of our generation! Dancing and singing helps calm the nervous system and stimulate the vagus nerve.

Want to go deeper? On my website, I offer a free course named "Resurrect the Nervous System." This course is self-led and short, but so, so effective in getting participants to recognize their own nervous system dysregulation, learn how to manage it, and self-regulate in everyday life. Check it out at www.deniseconde.com. Again, it's *free*!

Whenever you feel your body entering a dysregulated state, remember this is just a feeling that has been stored in the body and that staying aware of this feeling is very important. Once the feeling has passed, describe (whether in a journal or just in your head) how your body felt in that moment. Did it feel numb? Or did it feel distinct sensations, such as heat coming up the neck and into the face, pressure in the chest and arms, a sudden knot in the stomach, "seeing red," hairs standing up on the back of the neck, or pressure in the head? Identifying the actual sensations your body is experiencing in these moments is fundamental to system regulation.

"Ugh! More feelings?" I hear you ask? Yes, more feelings! The purpose of this is to feel the sensation and to take note of when you feel it coming and building; to pause. Even better if you can take that moment to feel *all* the sensations in your body.

Don't let the feeling own you with a kneejerk reaction and words that you might later regret. These responses are always a choice. In that moment when all the sensations are coming in and bubbling up, there's a moment—a pause—where you get to choose whether you react from a place of anger from the past or whether you respond calmly from the present. It will serve you well to choose to observe the feeling and sensation and stay put as an observer of your own body. Respect the pause that comes during emotion recognition.

If it gets too much, leave the conversation or situation. Announce that you are feeling upset and need a moment, and that you will come back in ten minutes. "Just leave?" you ask? Yes! Take ten minutes to identify and name the sensations. Breathe deeply in through your nose and out of your mouth until you've calmed your nervous system. This is an opportunity for growth, so use it wisely.

Triggers are your biggest teachers. Once you have identified the sensations that accompany your dysregulation, you can say to yourself the next time they return, "A-ha! There you are! I choose what to do with this sensation and information. I choose how I want to respond. I can honor myself."

Again, if this sensation is overwhelming and you don't feel you can respond in a productive manner, remove yourself from whatever you're doing, for your own integrity and for the sake of the person you are engaging with (if anyone). Honor yourself first in your valor.

It takes great courage to decide to feel your less pleasant emotions and bodily sensations, and it is for this reason that I think this method is just gorgeous. It is why it is my gift to you!

The Magic of Meditation

It took me a year to embrace the idea of meditation. Before that, I rejected it. I was already journaling and doing yoga. How much more did I really need to do? "I'm not some Buddhist monk, nor am I going to become one," my ego said. Indeed, your ego will buck and rage at the idea of you adding something new to your routine, and will try to convince you that you don't need any new practices in your life. I listened to my ego for way too long.

Still, I became curious at some point, and decided to give it a try.

I started meditating by lying down in my bed, covered with a comfy blanket. I was completely flat, with no pillow under my head. (I still lie down when I meditate. There's no right or wrong way to do it.)

There are so many free guided meditations all over the Internet and YouTube that I still use today. I started with an hour-long sound bowl guided meditation that included open-mouthed breathing, and this meditation literally changed the way I started feeling inside my body.

I still may not be a Buddhist monk, but I have a deep appreciation for what meditation and breathwork have done for me. When I started my meditation and breathwork journey, I had my daughters' schedules to keep up with, my job, places to go, and people to see. Yet, I was now on a path that was committed to my growth and healing. I was the leader in my own life. I carved out these moments just for me, just like you have by reading this book. (Congratulations, new self-leader and self-healer!)

You only get this one life, so start making more choices that center around your own needs and regulate your nervous system. Schedule time on a calendar for yourself so everyone around you knows this time is for you. I know you have a calendar, whether digital or physical, so you have no excuse! A former colleague of mine suggested that I put my yoga time on the family schedule so everyone else was aware of it, and it was when she made this simple recommendation that I realized, for the very first time, that we had a calendar for every kind of task *except those dedicated to taking care of me.*

Is this the case for you, too?

Pick something that you want to do to help regulate your nervous system and book it into your calendar. Scheduling in my yoga time felt selfish at first, but I was surprised at how quickly my husband and kids embraced it and celebrated the fact that I was taking time for myself.

By the way, when those around you celebrate you wanting to take care of yourself, note who they are. Those are your people. Also take note of the ones that make fun of it or reject it, but understand that their rejection or judgment is about them, not you. You do you, my love, and don't give a fuck about what others think. Don't try to convince others and overexplain. Be okay with being misunderstood. Get out there, have some fun, and start returning that gorgeous, sexy nervous system of yours to homeostasis!

2

Subconscious Behavioral Patterns and Conditioning

*E*ASY ON ME BY ADELE fits well into this chapter. Many of us were once children who weren't able to choose what they wanted to do. The best part about being an adult is the fact that we have choice in everything we do. Everything! Unfortunately, subconscious behavioral patterns and the way some of us were conditioned keeps us from growing, even when we have the best intentions. Play this song while reading this chapter.

Now we've learned all about the nervous system, let's spend some time talking about the conscious and subconscious. Easy, right? For someone as smart as you are, absolutely.

The first thing you need to understand is, all the messages that the brain receives are carried away from the brain and to the rest of the body via the "motor pathway." This can be broken down into two parts. The first part of the motor pathway is the somatic (voluntary) part, which is also known as the conscious part of the brain. It is our perception of the world. The second part is the autonomic (involuntary) part, also known as our subconscious. This is where everything we have learned to think and feel about ourselves is stored. Whether it's the truth or a lie, the subconscious absorbs it all and interprets everything it observes as "normal."

The conscious is the "thinking" part of the brain. In the conscious, we can reason while also taking in information from our outer world through the senses (touch, sight, smell, hearing, and taste), or the "sensory pathway."

We're going to focus on the subconscious here. Between ninety and ninety-five percent of our thinking occurs in the subconscious mind. With this in mind, consider how much you are actually operating from your own beliefs and behaviors.

Subconscious Behavioral Patterns

Everything you've ever been told and taught from the time you were born until now is stored in your subconscious. This is the involuntary part of your nervous system that allows you to drive to work and back without you having to consciously think about it. This is also where those behavioral patterns that no longer serve you lie. They are ingrained in your subconscious and have likely been normalized since your childhood. In other words, this is where all the horrible things you've been told about yourself are housed; the things that you've heard so often that you now believe them.

While we were discussing the nervous system in Chapter 1, we explored what it means to live in survival mode ("fight," "flight," "freeze," or "fawn"). To break the states of survival mode down a little, "fight" means standing there and arguing back, "flight" means removing yourself from the situation, "freeze" means staying put and not knowing what to do or say, and "fawn" means people-pleasing or saying what you think the other person wants to hear. The activation of survival mode takes place in the autonomic (involuntary) nervous system, meaning that these responses ("fight," "flight," "freeze," and "fawn") are involuntary, based on what's going on outside of you.

These states are normal, and your body will oscillate in and out of these states during day-to-day life. The key is becoming conscious about which nervous system state you might be in at a given point in time.

All of this is to say that when you are in survival mode, you are running on a subconscious pattern of behavior you've learned. What is a subconscious pattern, you ask? It is a record of the past. Essentially, you have been conditioned to act and behave in a certain way in order to receive love.

The subconscious doesn't just contain your trauma responses; it clings onto everything you've learned in life that you consider to be true. These are the things you've been conditioned to like and not like (down to even the food you eat), the language you speak, and your work ethic; they are your beliefs about money, how to raise a child, the way you should and shouldn't dress, your body, marriage, divorce, love, and more. All of this is set on autopilot and has been under construction since you were born. Because of this, you often believe (and even become) what you are told.

John Mayer sings in *Daughters* (my fellow Gen Xer who gets it!) about how daughters will repeat their mothers' and fathers' subconscious patterns of how to live and love. He reminds us that these subconscious patterns that were formed in early childhood have nothing to do with our present partners and children. Listen to this song several times.

To summarize, many of the beliefs that you have were passed onto you by others, and therefore *don't belong to you*. This means you can change anything you want about yourself. You can build a new subconscious and self-image. You get to choose who you want to be every single day in every moment of your life, regardless of what others have said about you. You have amazing intelligence designed exactly for this purpose built into your brain; you just have to unlock its potential.

This means diving deeper into the subconscious. Specifically, it means examining your caregivers' behavioral patterns so you can establish how deep into the subconscious your learned behaviors are buried. If you don't do this, you won't be able to unearth your behavioral patterns and identify who exactly you no longer want to be.

Is this what vulnerability looks like? Hell yeah!

It's also important to focus on the good stuff that you discover during this process, too — the stuff you want to keep; the stuff that you like about yourself.

As difficult as this may be, remember that the discomfort that comes with growing and learning about yourself is a symptom of self-development, *not* a sign that you should give up.

If you're anything like me, you won't want to sit down with a counselor and rehash all the horrible things that happened to you as a child and an adult, nor will you want to admit to the horrible things *you* have said and done as an adult. There's still a stigma associated with therapy and asking for help; individuals may be fearful of being placed in a box through their being diagnosed with addiction, depression, anxiety, complex PTSD, and so on. (By the way, recent research indicates that if Gen Xers received such diagnoses in their twenties, thirties, and even early forties, their symptoms usually stemmed from childhood trauma or from dysfunctional or abusive relationships in adulthood. Therefore, this solo work I'm guiding you through in this book can form a gentle introduction to self-help and self-healing without the use of a therapist.) I am grateful that I did the work while seeing a counselor (and then a mentor, whose guidance exponentially increased my subconscious growth) when I felt ready to. This, for me, marked the beginning of me taking ultimate responsibility for my life and actions, and was my first step toward making the changes I so desperately wanted to make in my life.

The point is that there are many options when it comes to healing your subconscious, and the choice of where you seek guidance from is yours.

Trauma Reenactment

Many of us have a difficult time with looking at our lives and traumas objectively, and we therefore fall into the vicious cycle of reenacting the traumas we were subjected to as children. Your ego will keep you thinking you had a "perfectly normal" childhood and that *you* are the one that is flawed, but the apple won't ever fall far from the tree if you don't take a serious, honest look inside yourself and your family's trauma-based patterns. Dr. Nicole LePera and Dr. Bessel van der Kolk refer to such realizations as the "dark night of the soul" (you may recall this from the Preface). Brené Brown says:

> Owning our story can be hard, but not nearly as difficult as spending our lives running from it. Embracing our vulnerabilities is risky, but not nearly as dangerous as giving up on love and belonging and joy — the experiences that make us the most vulnerable. Only when we are brave enough to explore the darkness will we discover the infinite power of our light.[2]

---

[2] Sourced from brenebrown.com. Please see https://brenebrown.com/art/24339

I think we all start out afraid of changing (like Stevie Nicks sings in *Landslide*) when we've built our lives around our parents. Give that song a listen when thinking on your subconscious behavioral patterns.

As children, there is no doubt that many of us were once victims of our circumstances. We didn't get to choose many of the things that happened to us. However, staying in a "victim" mindset in adulthood can perpetuate the self-fulfilling prophecy that we have no control over our lives. While adults are certainly not immune to falling victim to dysfunctional or abusive relationships, there does need to be a balance of self-responsibility in the roles we play in adulthood. Therefore, analyzing the roles you're playing in your closest relationships right now should allow you to see whether you have put yourself in a "victim" mindset, and should also give you the opportunity to divorce yourself from this mindset.

Something to note: your closest, most intimate relationships are often the ones in which you are triggered the most, because of your core wounding. Core wounding is described as:

> …having a parent who denies your reality, having a parent who does not see or hear you, having a parent who vicariously lives through you or attempts to mold and shape you, having a parent who does not model boundaries, having a parent who is overly focused on appearance, [and/or] having a parent who cannot regulate their emotions.[3]

Do any of these core woundings resonate with you? If so, circle them.

Many of us maintain our careers with ease but have a less-than-stellar track record with our personal relationships. So, whenever you feel

---

[3] LePera, N. (2021): *How to Do the Work*. Harper Wave (p.p. 60–63).

triggered while you're engaging with those who are closest to you, remember to feel the sensations in your body and to let them pass. Respect the pause and observe the bodily sensations that accompany it. You can respond with kindness and unconditional love, or you can react from a dysregulated nervous system and core wounding from the past. It's your choice.

Remember that this takes practice, just like any other skill. It all starts with you first being honest with yourself about the behaviors that are keeping you in the same place in your mind and life. Write them down. Remember, these behaviors are rooted in a story in your head that plays over and over like a 45 record. The story brings back the feelings you felt when that negative thing happened. End this cycle by acknowledging the story and the behavioral patterns that keep you feeling the same way you do about yourself, and then make the decision to no longer give your energy to the story. Let it go. It's in the past, and it's not something you can magically go back and change. Then, write a new, beautiful story in your subconscious about your future self. Write how you want to feel. Close your eyes. Envision yourself in your new life. Watch the way you're talking and smiling and moving. Describe it in as much detail as possible. Put on some relaxing background music. You and your mind are amazingly powerful tools, and you have the power to change what's occurring in your life. The subconscious might wield great influence over our lives, but it is also malleable like Play-Doh and can be changed, just like the wires of the nervous system. Imagine how that would feel. Describe all the feelings that would bring you: happiness; excitement; strength; motivation; freedom; power; inspiration; creativity; determination; brilliance; invigoration; beauty… Fall in love with these feelings, because the feeling is what controls it all: the body, mind, brain, nervous system, subconscious, and conscious.

To illustrate this process of self-analysis and make it feel a little more manageable, let's use me as a case study. Here is my assessment of my behavioral patterns versus my parents'.

MY PARENTS	ME
Beat me with a belt, grabbed me by the throat and threw me up against the wall/door, smacked me across the face hard enough for me to get a bloody nose, and grabbed me by the hair and threw me across the room, along with many more repeated physical attacks.	Spanked my youngest daughter when she was young, grabbed my oldest daughter by the throat in her early teenage years, and yelled at my daughters consistently.
Consistently yelled and screamed about money and paying bills.	Discussions about money consistently turned into a screaming match with my husband or were avoided altogether.
Denied or minimized how hurtful their actions were. Called me names (e.g., "whore," "loser," "stupid," "bitch," "weak," "alcoholic," "ungrateful") with no apology.	Minimized my daughters' realities and how hurtful my actions were. Called them names (e.g., "spoiled," "ungrateful brats," "bitches").
Perpetuated a consistent stream of conflict and chaos within the family unit.	Perpetuated a consistent stream of conflict and chaos within the family unit.

The deeper I went into my parents' past behaviors, the more I could see that I was bringing the same or similar behaviors and problems to my relationship with my husband and daughters. It was horrifying. I wanted to crawl under a blanket and hide from all the horrible things I'd said and done to my ex-husband, current husband, and daughters. The lyrics from *Iris* by The Goo Goo Dolls do a good job of explaining my deep feelings of mortification. I didn't want anyone to see me and certainly didn't think anyone would understand who I realized I had become.

My ego wanted so badly to keep it all inside. I didn't want to have to admit to the damage I'd done, and I certainly didn't know how to repair it all. I wanted to blame my husband, and this defensive line of thought led me to deflect and think that it was *him* who needed to take responsibility for his side of the street in our marriage. This, of course, was just me trying to take the limelight off myself as a coping mechanism. Sure, he had many behavioral patterns he needed to work on too, but they were for him to come to terms with, not me. Remember, you can't force anyone to make changes until they are ready to. Heal yourself first, my love.

I'd like to take a moment to send my love to those who have been repeatedly traumatized or who have been in dysfunctional relationships over long periods of time. My heart sees you and feels you. These experiences inflame the reptilian part of the brain and keep you stuck in the "fight" response, which causes a great deal of internal rage that unconsciously spills outward. In particular, narcissistic abuse and emotionally immature parents create a breeding ground for internal anger and rage that henceforth lies in wait, spoiling to be unleashed and leaving you easily triggered. This is why it's imperative to end a relationship with a narcissist as fast as possible and to identify whether you are also bringing dysfunction to your closest relationships. (We'll speak about narcissism in more depth in Chapter 4.)

As you saw in the "My Parents versus Me" table, I once grabbed my oldest daughter by her throat during a heated argument. I had never done this before (and never did again), and that devastating moment for me and her has been something I've had to sit with for a long period of time. I've had to reflect on it in some depth so I could understand myself and why I ever did such a thing. It's no coincidence that both my parents grabbed me by the throat during my teenage years and my early twenties — and that I then snapped into a trauma reenactment decades later.

Trauma reenactment occurs when an individual hasn't resolved childhood trauma, thus keeping that trauma alive inside the subconscious mind and body. The body is meant to keep itself safe, so a traumatized individual may disassociate from childhood trauma for decades until one day, it rears its ugly head.

I share this vulnerable moment with you so you can understand yourself a little better if you have unresolved childhood trauma. Be gentle on me and yourself. If you've done something similar, I've got you. Throughout this process, give yourself the unconditional love and self-compassion you need. Keep your nervous system regulated and pour on the self-love and self-forgiveness. Literally tell yourself that you forgive yourself; that you are learning and growing; that your heart is held; that you can move forward. What happened to you is not your fault, but it *is* your responsibility to heal and become conscious of your triggers and behaviors so you can grow into the "you" you've always dreamed of being.

Before I did the work, the pattern/behavior that played out the most for me, regardless of who I was married to, was as follows: I'd drink, a problem would be raised by someone I was close to, and I'd fall into a fit of rage (fight) or run away (flight).

I'm grateful my daughters were not around to witness those moments.

To view this objectively, this behavioral pattern is interesting: whenever my father drank (he quit when I was around nine years old), he also fell into fits of rage, which often included violence, screaming, and yelling.

Again, more trauma reenactment. Watered down, but still trauma reenactment.

For me, it didn't matter if I was with friends or my partner; these behaviors remained the same, from my teenage years and into adulthood. In other words, they'd been wired into my brain and subconscious. "Drinking, conflict, and chaos" was my program and pattern which had started with my father, which had started with *his* father. In other words, this program *wasn't mine, and I didn't need to tend to this pattern anymore.* I could take ultimate responsibility for my behavior and change it.

I have a completely different relationship with alcohol now, and I no longer use it as a coping mechanism. Instead, I feel my emotions and allow them to pass through me as they come, rather than being a vessel that carries everything locked deep inside, waiting for the magic of alcohol to give me the permission to unleash onto others everything that's ever hurt me.

As mentioned previously, most of us were raised to believe that addiction is a disease ("dis-ease"), yet this can sometimes overlook the blatant fact that it's often easy to trace substance abuse back to chronic nervous system dysregulation that was developed in childhood. Recognizing this allows us to take a deeper look into the nervous system and subconscious and evaluate whether we're using substances to "cope" with life, or whether we're creating a life that doesn't drive us to seek coping methods in the first place; a life that we are truly proud of and happy with.

Let's take my situation as an example. My father was a Vietnam veteran, and his behavioral patterns were often able to be explained in those terms (he suffered from PTSD). Yet (and I say this not to dismiss or devalue his valor from his time served) *before* my father went to Vietnam, there was an extremely high level of substance abuse (not to mention dysfunction, conflict, and chaos) among my father and his siblings. They fist-fought well into adulthood (and my siblings and I fist-fought in childhood as well). My father remained unaware of how his childhood and upbringing had been stored in his nervous system, and so many of his patterns went unrecognized — even relatively simple and "obvious" ones.

My mother, meanwhile, consistently created conflict and chaos among me and my siblings on family vacations and holidays. Remember, the dysregulated person will go looking for conflict or chaos, and if they come up empty, they will create the conflict or chaos they're looking for. There always had to be some sort of blowout, and I repeated this pattern into adulthood, albeit a watered down version of it.

I continued some of my father's other patterns, too: he was always rushing out the door searching for keys and blaming someone else for his tardiness. I, too, was always running out the door to work or an appointment, leaving everyone on pins and needles as they waited to see whether I would lose my cool or make it calmly out the door.

Again, the patterns that you've learned were never yours, and you get to choose how you live your life. Identify and decide which behaviors no longer serve you and act from there. And remember, keep the good stuff; the qualities that make you, you. There are many qualities that I have subconsciously inherited from my parents that are beautiful, and those behaviors and patterns need to be examined, too.

Are you celebrating the beautiful parts of yourself? If not, start now! Write a list of all the beautiful attributes that you have. Write it in this book or on a separate piece of paper.

MY PARENTS	ME
Had a strong work ethic, with perseverance and grit.	Has a strong work ethic, with perseverance and grit.
Was caring and loving.	Gives unconditional love.
Enjoyed dancing and music.	Enjoys dancing and live music.
Gave to our community through volunteering.	Went into teaching to serve kids; is now in service to adults.
Brought fun and laughter.	Brings fun and laughter.

Conditioning and the Roles We Play

Now that we've spoken about behavioral patterns, let's talk about conditioning.

Conditioning is the process that takes place when you figure out how you must change your behavior if you are to receive love. Who you grew up around conditioned you, for the better or worse, on how to receive love and what role you should play within your family. If your caretakers were emotionally dysregulated, you probably "changed hats" whenever needed in order to receive love, rather than just consistently staying true to yourself and wearing the same "hat" (your hat of valor) no matter what the situation was.

For me, I played the role of "the life of the party" most of the time, as well as the role of the "yes person." I was a people-pleaser. It took an especially long time for me to recognize the people-pleaser within myself and to admit to myself that I also played the role of "victim" and "rescuer/protector" as I saw fit.

While healing can be an extremely lonely walk at times and many of us have been conditioned to do everything on our own, know that you are *not* alone in this journey. If you're a Gen Xer, then I've got you! My clients have identified how they were conditioned, learned about the inner child archetypes, learned how to reparent themselves, and identified their core values so they can live with authenticity. You can travel that same path by actioning everything we're talking about in this book and seeking out a mentor, if needed.

Recognizing the role you played as a child (and still play into adulthood) to receive love from your parents (and partners) is important when you're on a journey to identifying who you are and who you want to be. Specifically, you must identify the things that you do in your relationships that cause you to betray or deceive yourself. Do you "pick your battles" and convince yourself that it "could be worse?" Do you overcommit or say yes to things that you really don't want to do, in fear that if you say no, the other person will make you feel guilty or you will not receive the love you are seeking? Do you overexplain or lie about why you can't do the thing?

If your "no" leads to a person becoming triggered and dysregulated, or if you just struggle to say "no," boundaries are most definitely needed. Boundaries are a necessary part of life, as scary as they may be to begin putting into place. Doing so is equivalent to saying "no" with a period, not with an apology or a reason. You can say, "I can't make it." "I'm not available." "That's not for me." You are not required to attend every event you're invited to, and you don't owe anyone an explanation—even your family members.

The Beauty of Boundaries

Take a few minutes to think about the boundaries you need in your life right now. Write them down on a piece of paper, and then create them.

Boundaries allow you to keep others in your life *and* honor yourself. They are not a reflection of the other person (even though others may tell you that's how they feel), but are a way for you to maintain your integrity, valor, and commitment to yourself. Just be careful that your boundaries don't become walls. Boundaries are there to bring balance, peace, and harmony to your relationships. If you realize that a relationship is completely dysfunctional and abusive and that you need to go "no contact" with them, then by all means, build the wall and keep it there. However, if the person in question is also willing to work on themselves, then discuss the new boundaries you'd like to create in your relationship. Love is a beautiful thing and can be worth fighting for.

The responsibility of filling the role that has kept you in the good graces of a family member is no longer a burden for you to carry. It kept you safe and served a purpose when you were younger, but now, it is time to let go of it.

3

Family Enmeshment
and Hierarchy Issues

A S WE BEGIN TO GAIN more awareness, it may seem too overwhelming to deal with. Listen to *Light of Love* by Florence & The Machine to ease your heart if it becomes troubled. We need the contrasts of life, and in this instance, we must go through the darkness to obtain the light within each of us.

Family Enmeshment

The topic of family enmeshment is pivotal for you to explore if you are to step into your valor. So, first, what is enmeshment?

Enmeshment is where no boundaries exist within a family unit. An enmeshed family is incapable of seeing things from another's perspective.

In an enmeshed family, we also develop loose mental/emotional boundaries, which result in a tendency to engage in groupthink. This happens when there is a group conceptualization of our thoughts and beliefs. [This] is particularly salient in religious households, where it's "understood" that everyone will follow the same practices and beliefs. The message, both direct and indirect, received by all family members, is one of conformity, accompanied by a fear of being ostracized for noncompliance.[4]

Maybe you've been told that your business is the rest of the family's business, too. In my case, if I went to my siblings for advice or about concerns relating to my parents, what I said always got back to my parents, and the same thing happened the other way around: if I shared anything with my parents about my marriage or my siblings, what I said always got back to the person to which my concerns had referred.

Basically, everyone knew everyone else's business, and the betrayal was astonishing. If you shared something, you could bet it would be the next day's gossip, plastered like the front-page headline on a newspaper. This was totally normalized.

Has this happened in your family? If so, I send you love.

I remember many occasions where my father called me and "spoke on behalf of the entire family." He would tell me that my actions affected everyone and that it didn't matter what I wanted because they weren't my choices to make. My mother also loved to talk about my sisters and victimize herself because "her adult daughters were living their own lives and making decisions she didn't agree with." She'd talk about all their mistakes and take the "victimhood" stance, rather than solving her issues with my sisters on her own. This resulted in me and my sisters having

---

[4] LePera, N. (2021): *How to Do the Work*. Harper Wave (p. 187).

very little chance to have autonomous relationships with one another outside the family drama and dynamics. The chaos and conflicts became our only point of connection. This also meant that I learned to depend on my friends (rather than my sisters and parents) for comfort and safety from a very early age. I knew I would be betrayed by my sisters and that what I shared with them about my parents would eventually get back to my parents and be brought back up for years to come.

I do not share all of this so I can villainize my family. I would participate in this behavior at times, too. It was a means of receiving love and acceptance within the family unit. My sisters betrayed me and I betrayed them, because we felt this was the easiest way to receive love from our parents; to be the golden child of the moment; to be the one that felt less fucked up than the sibling being discussed. It reassured me that my mother must think highly enough of me to share her "concerns" with me, even though I knew, deep down, that she'd be talking behind my back about me to my siblings the first chance she got. This also meant that when I finally asked my mother for boundaries at the age of forty-seven, it enraged her. She told me that *she* was the mother and that *she* set the boundaries, not me. From this point, her behavior only worsened, which led to me cutting off all contact. I needed to heal. My marriage needed to heal. My daughters needed to heal. That burning desire to stop the constant family drama, dysfunction, and chaos reached its climax. I finally realized that while I couldn't change anyone else, I *could* change myself, and that I had the power to end the generational enmeshment and family dysfunction; to give myself, my husband, and my daughters a healthier and happier life.

You have that power, too!

Your parents, operating from their ego, might regularly lecture you about your shortcomings, the mistakes you've made, and the habits or coping mechanisms you've developed, to push you right back to where they are comfortable with you being, and to keep you playing the role they want you to play within the family unit. This keeps the chaos and conflict of the family going (remember that dysregulated people seek chaos and conflict).

The other members of your family may tell you that you don't deserve better treatment. Things like, "Who do you think you are?" or, "We are the [insert your last name here] and this is how we do things!" can be translated to, "Conform to the groupthink or perish."

Loyalty to a dysfunctional family is deeply rooted in the normalization of destructive behaviors and emotional immaturity. When this is all you've known, these behaviors feel like home. When a child is unconditionally loyal to their family (even into adulthood) to keep themselves safe and loved and accepted, they feel a false sense of safety and security ("false" because safety comes from healthy relationships).

I'm here to tell you that while you most definitely needed your parents in order to survive as a child, you're now no longer required to participate in their circus. To overcome this dependency, your fear of rejection needs to be trumped by your need and want to heal yourself.

Bottom line: you are not responsible for your parents, including their emotions and behaviors. You are responsible for yourself and your children (so long as they are still minors, that is), and that's it. You choose who you are and who you want to be, regardless of the past and the things others may continue to say about you. No one defines you but you. *You* define you. Most importantly, you deserve unconditional love. If you've been receiving the message, "Fit in the box or you can't be loved," actively tell yourself, "I will fit in no one's box and love myself."

You are no longer a child. You no longer need their approval. Truly. It's not your job to keep the family's dysfunctional secrets. Eventually, the lock needs to be busted open, and I'm here to give you the key.

Do you want the key? Here it is!

To break this down further, let's look at the different types of enmeshment.

Parentification

Parentification is a type of enmeshment where a parent-child relationship is reversed in certain ways. The child becomes the parent to their parent, to meet the adult's emotional needs. This happens when a parent is emotionally immature.

This typically occurs:

- When there is an abusive/dysfunctional relationship or a divorce.
- When a parent or sibling is disabled or chronically ill.
- When there is parental drug or alcohol abuse.
- When there is a family dynamic where the older kids are expected to be the caregiver to the younger kids.
- When there is the death of a sibling or parent.

There are also many other examples of situations in which parentification can occur. Of course, feel free to add other examples here if this resonates with you.

- When the child is expected to function as a therapist to resolve issues among siblings on behalf of the parent (this is triangulation).
- When the child feels overly responsible for the parent's emotions and feelings.
- When the child is placed in between adults to serve as a referee.
- When the adult shares details with the child about their personal hardships, with the expectation that the child will counsel the parent, lend emotional support, or pick sides (if relevant).

- When the child takes on most of the adult's responsibilities, such as cooking, cleaning, or running an entire household (this does not include singular chores that are intentionally delegated by an adult).
- When the child has to listen to a parent complain and criticize extended family members (the child usually develops similar views as a result).
- When the child is consistently forced to help a sibling with their homework and be their caretaker.
- When the child is forced into the role of "protector" for the parent.
- When the child becomes overly self-reliant and hyper-independent.
- When the child becomes hypervigilant, constantly monitoring the parent's emotional state, to keep the peace.

Circle any of the items you have experienced.

Many Gen Xers were put in the position of "caregiver" to their parents and siblings. This still may be happening within your family of origin. Understand that playing such a role well into adulthood (or at all) is not healthy. You need to acknowledge and build awareness around parentification if you are to heal from it and not repeat these dynamics with your own children. This involves you grieving the loss of a childhood that you may not have had, learning to play again, carving out time for joy (to rebuild what may have been lost), placing boundaries so you can meet your own needs, and understanding that adults can handle being told "no."

As someone who has been parentified, you may identify as an "empath," because you were sensitive to everyone else's energy and needs when you were growing up. To you I say, it's not your job to "please" and counsel everyone around you. You can offer kindness and compassion to your parents, but a sense of balance still needs to be struck here.

Of course, your parents probably didn't know any better. Still, you must look at how this enmeshed codependency is affecting your life. You also need to accept that you cannot parent your parents, and that their lack of emotional maturity isn't for you to "fix" or to "save," no matter how much you may love them.

Begin to set limits around what you are comfortable with giving your time to and examine your intentions behind your "giving" this time away. Are you doing it out of obligation? Because it's something you've always done? What feelings are you left with after you "give" in this way? Anxiety? Anger? Resentment? Guilt? Shame? Exhaustion? How are you betraying your own needs and wants within your family of origin and intimate relationships in this respect? Seriously think about it.

You have the freedom to change these dynamics any time you wish, and if you need help doing so, I'm here for you!

Triangulation

I am the youngest in my family, and my oldest sister is six years older than me. When she was sixteen years old, I was ten. That's a *huge* gap in perception and maturity. When we each reflect on our childhoods, this difference is incredibly evident.

Perception issues, codependency, and parentification often lead to sibling rivalries, resentments, and a great deal of misunderstanding. There is often a hierarchy issue at play here, too. For example, if the oldest or older children were given permission to parent/discipline their younger siblings in childhood, they may attempt to continue this even into adulthood. There may be unresolved and unconscious resentment for both siblings in this situation, or the older sibling may continue to echo their parents' complaints about their younger sibling or vice versa.

If this is you, I send you love, as this is enmeshment at its finest! More specifically, this is triangulation.

I want you to remember that if a parent has a problem that needs to be resolved with their adult child, that's *their* responsibility, not yours or your sibling's. Boundaries need to be built around what you will be available for with regards to a parent complaining about your sibling (or the other parent, or anyone else in the family). Your parent's choice to confide in you about these things doesn't indicate that you have a magical friendship; it indicates that they are emotionally immature and codependent on you.

In homes with multiple siblings, each sibling usually gets a different version of their parents. This could be due to their parents' subconscious beliefs about how an older child versus a younger child should be expected to behave, the health of the parents' marriage, divorce, or how much money the parents were able to make during each child's upbringing. Regardless, each sibling's perspective and reality of what they experienced can look vastly different, and all those experiences need to be honored.

If you're the older sibling, please know that it wasn't your job to parent/discipline your younger sibling then (regardless of if your parents gave you permission to do so) and it certainly isn't now. If you are still "parenting" your adult siblings, stop. They are adults now. Build a friendship with your sibling instead. Go on fun outings together. Make a pact to move the relationship into the future, rather than living in the conditioned past.

If you're the younger sibling and your siblings still view you as a "little kid" rather than the adult you are, there is a hierarchy issue at play.

The order of your birth does not make anyone more or less deserving of love and respect. You are not somehow more or less human based on your order of birth.

Read that sentence again and underline it, because your ego may be telling you otherwise.

As a sibling, was your ego fed by a parent that sent you the message that since you are the oldest, that means you are somehow superior to your younger siblings? Or, as the youngest in the family, were you called "the baby?" Does this messaging still exist within your family? I hate to break it to you, but your siblings are your peers. They may have different life experiences and perceptions of your childhood and the world than you, but that doesn't suggest any inferiority or naivety on their part. Those perceptions and experiences are valid, and they need to be respected.

Ask yourself how your actions from the past (and even the present day) caused/cause harm to your sibling. Don't self-blame or -shame for this; you probably acted in this way to receive love, approval, or acceptance from a parent. Do you mirror the same beliefs about your sibling as your parents because your sibling did something back in 1980 that you believe still defines them as a person today? If so, own it, apologize, and move on. We all grow, make mistakes, and change. None of us are "kids" anymore. Let's start treating our siblings as the adults they are, with the love and respect they deserve.

If you have unresolved resentment toward a sibling who was positioned to be a caretaker for you (or you for them), take this moment to acknowledge that this wasn't your or their fault and that it is now time to change the dynamics within the relationship, without involvement from your parents or any other siblings. You are allowed to have autonomous relationships that exist on their own, outside other siblings' and your parents' involvement; a healthy relationship with boundaries and respect.

If the sibling in question cannot see your perspective or lacks understanding about family enmeshment, then unfortunately, that is their stuff to work through. Buy them this book! Remember, you aren't here to save everyone else or to convince someone else of your worth. Your focus must be on you, your partner, and your children if you are to break the cycles in your life.

Spousification

Spousification is similar to parentification and is a type of enmeshment where a parent treats their child as their spouse. This occurs when there is the death of a parent (even in adulthood), there is a divorce, or you otherwise have a single parent. Perhaps during your childhood, there was an absent parent and you were made to fill their place as the "man" or "woman" of the house.

Spousification is a passive form of emotional abuse. It is a codependent relationship where the adult depends way too much on their child for emotional support (and sometimes even financial support). This could also manifest as the adult showering the child with physical contact that is more appropriate for an intimate relationship. This could include tickling, a smack on the butt, or sitting the child on their lap after the child has hit their teenage years or become an adult.

There are little to no boundaries in this type of relationship, physical or emotional.

A child may feel guilty for the state of their parent's emotional wellbeing and their loneliness, especially if the child is told that the parent is choosing to not pursue another relationship because "they want to focus solely on the child, because their children are their world." This sets kids up to believe that the parent is giving everything up (including intimate adult relationships) to satisfy the needs of their children first, and this belief creates a lot of guilt in the children.

While this relationship may at first glance look like a close and healthy relationship between a parent and child, it's not. The dynamic may be unconscious and unintentional on the parent's part, but it still stands that there is a role reversal at play, whereby the child is expected to fulfill the role of a spouse.

This can also happen between a parent and child even when the parents are still married, *if* the parents have a very unhealthy marriage that lacks emotional or physical intimacy. In this situation, a parent can develop a codependent relationship with their child (rather than looking to repair their unhealthy marriage). Here, the parent becomes overly involved and dependent on the child well into the child's adulthood, and can seem like a helicopter parent.

Indeed, while spousification is often associated with childhood, it can easily happen in adulthood, too, particularly when there is the death of a parent and the other parent is widowed.

On that note: if you are a Gen Xer right now, your parents are probably aging, so when your parent loses their life partner, be careful not to attempt to fill the role of the deceased parent. You cannot fill that hole in their heart. It is common for the children of, say, a widowed mother to invertedly start "dating" their own mother — that is, to start taking her to all the places she would have gone to with her husband and fulfilling some of the roles he would have filled.

If one of your parents has passed, consider, has your relationship with your partner or yourself changed or grown distant because you or your partner now "date" your or their grieving parent?

What we're talking about here is a codependent, enmeshed relationship. Partnerships become greatly fractured when a parent becomes the top priority for one of the parties over a long period of time.

It's normal to grieve the loss of a family member, but losing a life partner and losing a parent are two completely different things, and there's a vast difference between "being there" for your widowed parent and becoming overly responsible for their every want and need and inserting yourself into the role of husband or wife. If you recognize yourself in this and your marriage/partnership has greatly suffered, it's time to roll yourself out of this type of enmeshment. How? By giving your time back to your relationship with your partner and kids. There are many services available for the aging today so you can continue to play a healthy role within your family as a son or daughter, rather than as a spouse, parent, or healthcare provider.

Take care of you first. Take care of your partnership and children first. You deserve consistent time on your own with your partner, friends, and children. Create boundaries and balance in your valor.

Helicopter Parenting

Helicopter parenting is where the parent is constantly attempting to control their child through micromanagement. This involves them constantly worrying about their safety, having strict rules, always trying to solve every problem for the child, and getting overly involved in their child's academic, extracurricular, social, and romantic life. This parent may seem (and be) well-meaning, but they nonetheless project their anxieties and insecurities about the world onto their child.

There are no boundaries in this type of relationship. The parent is hypervigilant due to their own nervous system being in a constant state of dysregulation.

What are the effects of having a hypervigilant parent?

- The development of coping mechanisms such as gambling, overuse of alcohol/drugs, food, sex, and the other nervous system coping mechanisms discussed in Chapter 1.
- Anxiety or bouts of depression.

- Hating feeling controlled or micromanaged in your current life by anyone.
- Constantly feeling "stressed."
- Consuming yourself with work and hobbies.
- Doing anything to avoid a conflict or an uncomfortable conversation by changing the subject when confronted.
- Emotionally pushing others away.

If you recognize yourself as someone who experienced this or is still experiencing this into adulthood, congratulations! You've met yourself and now know how to begin regulating your nervous system and setting boundaries, and you have been granted permission to live an autonomous life. Your parents' worries and anxieties are no longer yours to carry. You are safe to navigate the world on your own. You can have hard conversations.

If you struggle to communicate in your relationships, Chapter 5 will help guide you through that. I've got you!

Hierarchy Issues

Perhaps you feel close to your parents or siblings — close enough to invite them into your relationship or parenting problems. Do you do this? If so, stop from hereon out. If you do not, you will be perpetuating a common hierarchy issue. (Note that this does not refer to those in abusive, manipulative, or otherwise seriously harmful relationships. If you think this could be you, seek professionals and a stable support system, family included. You are not alone.)

Your partner knows when you're discussing your marital issues with others (even if you think they don't), and this dishonors the relationship.

If you do this, your partner will feel that they stand in a "lesser" position in your life. Besides, using your relationship problems as a point of connection with others is emotionally immature.

Even if your adult siblings or parents do it, this is not okay. In fact, it's very damaging. This behavioral pattern will dampen the growth, intimacy level, and vulnerability within your relationship. It's psychologically damaging, and it crosses emotional boundaries.

So, who should you discuss your marital problems with? *Your partner,* with boundaries in place. This means that if your parents continually ask questions about your marriage, financial matters, or parenting style (or whatever it is), you need to honor and love yourself, your partner, and your children more than you wish to maintain any family enmeshment and hierarchies. This is emotional maturity, and this will help you to gain the emotional intelligence you need to step into your true self.

As another unspoken rule in a hierarchy, parents often think they have the "right" to tell their adult children how to parent. The ego of a parent might be triggered if you tell them that you want to parent in a way that's different from how *they* parented. From their ego's perspective, this could be interpreted as you questioning the way they parented you and you indicating that they didn't do a good job. Some conflicts may arise in this regard. But remember, boundaries are there to help you keep the people you love in your life while also giving yourself and your partner the love you both deserve. You have the right to parent the way you see fit, regardless of your parents' beliefs and paradigms.

Another hierarchy-based issue many Gen Xers face is one (or both) of their parents continually disrespecting their (as in, your) spouse, or making rude remarks about their partner in front of others (we'll be talking about a very specific category of such behavior in the next chapter). If this happens, do not ignore this. It is your responsibility to address the situation with boundaries and consequences for moving forward. You made a vow to honor your spouse when you entered a relationship with them, and allowing your partner to be abused or disrespected by your parent just because you're used to it isn't okay. Making excuses like, "They are old and won't change," or, "If I stand up to them, they'll say I'm choosing you over them," isn't good enough. You chose your spouse over your parents when you committed to them. That's part of being in a mature, loving relationship. It's immature to ignore your partner's needs, and you invalidate them as a person when you continue to allow them to be abused or disrespected by one of your parents.

If you are "afraid" to stand up to your parent and think it might lead you to being ostracized by your family, this is a huge indication that you are involved in a dysfunctional parent-child relationship. It also does not matter how old your parent is; trying to excuse their behavior away because you don't know how long you have left with your them (and asking your partner to "just ignore" the behavior on your behalf) is extremely damaging and emotional betrayal, not only to yourself, but to your partner.

Old age does not automatically mean respect is deserved. Love and respect must be mutual. What's more, exposing your children to a lack of mutual love and respect teaches them that adults are allowed to be abusive simply because they are older than them. You have the right to choose what your children are exposed to, and betraying yourself and your partner for the sake of a couple family gatherings a year is akin to you saying to your kids, "It's okay to put on a façade and play a role for the sake of pleasing your abuser."

No matter what age an adult is and no matter what their place in an age-old hierarchy, emotional immaturity, abuse, and disrespect are never okay. Yes, I know the old saying and conditioning is to "respect your elders." Us Gen Xers were also told that "respect is something to be earned." This was so ingrained into one of my clients that it was one of the first things she mentioned to me when we started working together. This conditioning had, for them, led to years and years of abuse from family members. I made it clear to that client (and I want to make it clear to you) that respect is a birthright. It's not something to be earned and it's certainly not something that is based on age or hierarchy. Just because someone is older than you and is "family" does not mean they have the right to disrespect you, your partner, or your children. A true family offers respect and love for each member. A true family celebrates the uniqueness of every stage of each member's life.

If you attempt to put a boundary in place and to call the abusive, disrespectful parent out on their mistreatment of you, your spouse, or your children, and they retaliate by saying that you are no longer welcome at family gatherings (a common reaction, unfortunately), this may hurt deeply. However, this is what it takes to be a generational-cycle-breaker and to realign another generation.

Ask yourself, what are you allowing to happen in your life? How are you betraying your own wants and needs in your most intimate relationships, all because of "family" and the hierarchies of those who came before you? How can you place boundaries around your relationship with your family members and honor yourself, your partner, and your children? How can you create a healthier relationship with yourself and your partner and validate your and your partner's feelings? Write these questions down on a piece of paper and answer them honestly. You've got this, and I believe in you!

Going "no contact" or "low contact" with family members that emotionally abuse you allows your kids to see what appropriate behavior is and isn't. Stop normalizing their grandparents' or other family members' outbursts and judgmental/criticizing behavior. This is your life, and you should never want to betray yourself in front of your children in order to appease another family member. Otherwise, your kids will learn to do exactly the same in life: they will miss the red flags of others in their personal relationships, because mistreatment by others has become so normalized.

It is also important to allow your kids to have their own boundaries with family. If they feel uncomfortable around a grandparent, aunt, or uncle, don't force them to hug and kiss them, and tell the person in question that they are being disrespectful if they try to force these things onto your child. Relationships are built over time through trust, not because of the fact of someone being "family," so forcing kids to hug and kiss and have relationships with people they are uncomfortable with teaches them to betray themselves and their own intuition about people. Honor how they feel and let them know they have a right to choose who touches them and takes up their personal space.

Think about that time when you were forced to physically engage with a "family" member that you only saw during birthdays, weddings, and funerals. They knew nothing about you, but because you shared a bloodline, that somehow magically meant you were "family." This probably made you uncomfortable. Pause and give this some serious thought.

4

The Family Scapegoat

*I*N THE AIR TONIGHT BY Phil Collins is fitting for this chapter related to narcissism. The ominous tone, the power of the drums, and the lyrics set the stage for the deep dark feelings of what narcissism robs its victims of. Narcissists bring with them lies, gaslighting, and mental gymnastics, to name a few of their methods. I highly recommend playing this song in the background while reading this chapter.

Remember when I mentioned that my husband said that he didn't feel loved by me and that something had changed within me? He was right, but I knew I was no longer grieving my father's loss, so I couldn't understand why I was so numb inside. I knew this wasn't who I was.

During this time in my life, I was unconsciously experiencing narcissistic abuse on an extremely high level, and had been for four years. When my father passed, the "yin" to the "yang" of my parents' relationship also left, and my mother's narcissism went into full throttle.

To add insult to injury, my husband's father passed away just eight months before my own father's death. My husband and our children and

I were shrouded in grief and narcissistic abuse. Talk about God giving you all you can handle!

During this time, it felt like the air in the room and my very lifeforce were being sucked away. The mental anguish, guilt, and shame I harbored for not wanting my mother around in the wake of my father's death was torturous. Paralyzing, in fact.

I couldn't put my finger on why I felt the way I did; I just knew something was horribly "off" inside me. I experienced constant anxiety and depression, and was dissociated and easily angered when my mother was present (and immediately after visits).

Completely unaware of the cause of my feelings and dysregulation, I often drank alcohol to ease the anxiety and internal disturbances of my intuition. During my mother's visits, I was physically present, but my mind was elsewhere, seeking safety and waiting for the visit to end. Once it did, I would collapse into tears, heartbroken over the way I was belittled and over the godawful things my mother would say about my sisters, extended family, or close family friends.

I should note here that my mother wouldn't share these snippets of gossip with me to seek counsel on how to resolve the problems within her relationships. She would share them to degrade and demean others. She used these conversations as an opportunity to stomp on the beautiful souls who had supported her loss when my father died.

This behavior from my mother was nothing new. It was something I had raised with my sisters decades before, but (understandably — we were all entrenched in toxicity!) my concerns were brushed under the carpet, as were all the physical attacks we endured (and were continuing to endure).

My mother physically attacked my middle sister the day we laid my father to rest. I was forty-four years old at the time. This is the last attack I was told about since going "no contact." I pray for my sisters every day.

Reckoning With Narcissism in Others

There are many ways to identify a narcissist and the red flags that should not be ignored.

First and foremost, narcissists have an overly grandiose persona. They constantly crave attention and need to be celebrated for every decision they make. They want you to tell them (and to really feel) that every decision they make is the best and most righteous choice ever made, and they want you to make them the center of attention in the process.

If you disagree with the choices or opinions of a narcissist, there will be hell to pay—maybe not right at that exact moment, but at some point. You will be spoken over and belittled until the narcissist feels they've overpowered you and "won." At other times, they will make you feel like the best person in the world, love bombing you with gifts while simultaneously gossiping to you about and belittling everyone else in your life.

A narcissist may offer a shallow apology for their physically and emotionally violent behavior, but they will never truly take responsibility for any pain they cause. They may make some changes that last for a few weeks or months, but they will always ultimately readopt the same behaviors. I endured this for decades. From then, new tactics will be employed, such as the silent treatment, leaving you walking on eggshells and not knowing what to expect from day-to-day. They will accuse you of doing the exact things they have done repeatedly over the course of their lifetime, and they will go as far as to use money, vacations, and even your children to manipulate you.

To deepen this discussion, I wanted to share this Instagram post from Lynn Catalano, who I played soccer with during our childhood (our kids eventually became friends, too).[5] At one point in our friendship, we sat together watching our kids at sporting events. Little did I know that she was experiencing similar torment to what I was: narcissistic abuse. Her Instagram post said this:

> Most people are familiar with this overt narcissist who loves the spotlight, needs constant praise and adoration, and uses people for their benefit. But there's another kind of narcissist who does just as much damage, but in a different way.

Lynn wrote a book called *Wrecking Ball Relationships,* and she quoted her book in the next line of the Instagram post, stating:

> The most on-brand behavior that all covert narcissists share is their passive-aggressive behavior. Covert narcissists often portray themselves as the victim, showing contempt for everyone else. Like traditional narcissists, their behavior is a manifestation of their deep insecurities. They are masters of the microaggression, cloaking insults as slips of the tongue, oversights, or humor, giving their victims death by a thousand cuts. With covert narcissists, the hits keep coming, but they continue to act like the victim, using guilt and shame to collect attention.

This resonated with me so much, I had to share it.

A narcissist will feel your energy pulling away when you are starting to feel uncomfortable with their behavior. This "pulling away" will be

---

[5] Posted on July 28, 2022, by @wreckingballrelationships. [Instagram Post]. Please see www.instagram.com/p/Cgj0cZ_uccK

even more obvious when you have recently asked for improved or better treatment, to no avail. In this situation, the narcissist will blow up and turn the tables back on you, stating things like:

- "I don't have these problems with anyone else."
- "There's something wrong with you."
- "What did I even do?" (Insinuating they couldn't possibly do anything hurtful or have no idea what the problem is.)
- "Why do you need to keep bringing this up?"
- "You're so negative."
- "You're living in the past."
- "You're just jealous of me."
- "You're crazy."
- "You need help."

When you are involved with a narcissist in any capacity, triangulation is consistently at work. This is the process of (consciously or unconsciously) isolating one person as the target (often called the "scapegoat"). The "scapegoat" is usually the person who the narcissist thinks is the "weakest," or the easiest to manipulate. A narcissist will also often employ another person (the "flying monkey") to attack the target on their behalf while they sit back and watch the chaos unfold.

As an example of this, my mother was once talking to me about an occasion when my oldest sister had verbally attacked me. During the conversation, she said, "That's what you get when you poke the volcano," with a snide, proud smirk (meaning, she thought that I deserved the emotional reaction I got from my sister—the "volcano").

The "wrongness" of that comment instantly hit my body like a freight train. I remember thinking about it and discussing it with my husband afterwards, saying, "Who on this earth refers to one of their adult kids as a 'volcano' and takes great pride and joy in saying it?" My body and heart knew this was wrong on so many levels.

When two people get together and feel justified in one party claiming victimhood and the other party bullying others (usually the "scapegoat") in the "victim's" place, an insidious codependent relationship is at play. Better yet is when the narcissist tries to convince the target that they deserved what they got (like my mother's comment about my sister's outburst).

I don't care what the reason or explanation for you "deserving" to be screamed at and treated poorly is—no one deserves that! With an exclamation point! These are telltale signs of you being selected as a scapegoat, and this behavior is far from healthy or normal. Getting an adult child to attack another family member is akin to exploiting that adult child, and is abuse. Specifically, it is the abuse of the child being exploited (the "flying monkey") and the abuse of the child being attacked (the "scapegoat"). Even subtly using one sibling to speak to another sibling on behalf of a parent is emotional immaturity, manipulation, and triangulation.

When you are made into a "scapegoat," the narcissist will say and do anything to invalidate your feelings, avoid taking responsibility, and attempt to make you feel guilty (or even crazy) for addressing their behavior. Around and around the conversation will go. They will punish you for raising an issue and sharing your feelings by having a rage episode, or by inserting the "flying monkey" to "straighten you out." They will rage at a discussion around boundaries or boundaries will be ignored, and the manipulation and guilt will worsen at the mere mention of those boundaries. Smear campaigns will begin, the story often being riddled with lies and exaggerations. A narcissist is very bold and confident that others (such as the "flying monkey") will believe their lies, even if there are multiple people that could attest otherwise. Any unhealthy coping mechanisms of yours that have been observed by the narcissist will be exploited and used against you, to convince others that you are crazy, unstable, and not to not be taken seriously. Similarly, if you have been vulnerable with the narcissist and told them about the mistakes that you've made in any area of your life, they will use this information against you, going after your Achilles' heel while you're trying to run away, distance yourself, or go "low/no contact." Gaslighting will also take place, with downright denial of something they said (even in the moments right after they said it). The conversation will be twisted and turned back on those witnessing the statements with denial and "crazymaking." They will attempt to isolate you and will not stop until they are successful in this endeavor, causing you to doubt your truth and reality.

A narcissist will insert themselves into your life and will often try to get between you and your spouse by making belittling remarks about you to your spouse. A narcissist will even go as far as making sexual comments/gestures to your spouse in front of you, to attempt to draw a reaction from you and to make you feel as though you are being oversensitive. Once your spouse no longer "plays along" with the narcissist's love bombing, grand gestures, and attempts to inflate their ego, your spouse will be discarded by the narcissist, any pedestal your spouse was on will come crumbling down, and the "flying monkey" will come in to act on behalf of the narcissist. The narcissist and the "flying monkey" will paint a picture of your spouse, claiming that the narcissist was victimized by them and that the spouse was abusive toward the narcissist.

Have you been involved in this type of dynamic? If so, I'm here for you.

I'd like to direct you to a quote from Dana Morningstar's *Out of the Fog*. This is relevant regardless of how old you are or what stage of your life you are in.

Parents don't put their children in harm's way to get attention; predators do. Parents don't use, abuse or exploit their children in order to get their own self-esteem needs met: predators do.[6]

When Narcissists Turn to Grooming

In the aforementioned (very specific but very common) situation, the target and the target's spouse (if relevant) can become very tempted to expose the poisonous codependent relationship between the narcissist and the "flying monkey" for what it really is (if they haven't already). The narcissist, however, cannot allow themselves to be revealed — their relationship with the "flying monkey" is meant to be seen as healthy, normal, and wonderful — so they up the ante: the narcissist and the "flying monkey" begin devaluating the target and their spouse through the couple's children.

This covert operation of grooming the children and turning them against the target is a long game. It's slow and methodical. Here, the narcissist will attempt to insert the "flying monkey" into the target's children's life. If the target or the target's children reject this new relationship, new tactics must be employed; the narcissist will go to any lengths to "split" the target's children (if the target has more than one child). In this situation, the "flying monkey" will typically make a sudden appearance in one child's life to "show support" (even though they've never done so in the past) while the narcissist goes after another. If the narcissist is aware of any mistakes the target has made or of any unhealthy

---

[6] Morningstar, D. (2017): *Out of the Fog: Moving from Confusion to Clarity After Narcissistic Abuse*. Morningstar Media (p. 117).

coping mechanisms that they have, the narcissist will "shine a light on these for the children to see" during what are supposed to be fun outings with the narcissist. Before this, though, the narcissist will tell the children that they will keep the children's "secrets" and that they are there for them (in attempts to gain trust). The narcissist will give gifts (love bombing) and show clear favoritism to one of the target's children over the other children, to feed the child's ego. In return, they will use the child to "dig up dirt" on the target (to continue the narrative that the target is flawed, unworthy, and crazy, and that the children must be "saved"). This process is called grooming.

Healthy parents discuss their issues one on one with their adult children, with genuine concern and love. Healthy parents offer love and support and ways to help, without giving unsolicited advice or making attempts to manipulate, guilt, or shame. Healthy grandparents do not use their grandchildren for information or dirt on their parents. Healthy grandparents do not get in between a parent and child's relationship to turn the child against their own parent.

Narcissists tell the target's children's "secrets" to the "flying monkey" so they can be weaponized. The narcissist will tell lie after lie to justify the narrative they are feeding the target's children, the "flying monkey," or anyone else who will lend an ear. They tell these lies through the lens of them (the narcissist) being a savior.

The Effects of Reckoning With Narcissism in Others

I took anti-anxiety pills for a while after my father died because I was so angry and full of anxiety due to my mother's narcissistic behavior. I secretly knew that the only way I could tolerate being around my mother and sister was if I was drugged, numbed, and quiet. I felt this was the only way I could keep myself safe and "in control."

Eventually, I developed a tremor in my neck that made my head physically shake, like how you would shake if you were cold, or how a traumatized, beaten animal shakes. This tremor is something I still occasionally deal with, especially when I'm highly stressed. My jaw was also constantly clenched, my shoulders were raised toward my ears, and my knees became so inflamed that I could barely walk.

Your body will begin to show physical symptoms if you are subjected to repeated trauma and abuse. Notice these signs.

At the time, my doctor just thought I was going through the normal grieving process, and he recommended that I stop using my anxiety medication so I could allow my body to process my grief naturally. This turned out to be good advice (though not for the reason the doctor thought). I know now that if I had stayed on that medication, I wouldn't have been able to identify the trauma and abuse I was surrounded by. It simply would have continued. Once I came off the medication that was numbing me, however, I became cognizant of the continued dysfunction around me.

Being in a relationship with a narcissist and a "flying monkey" over an extended period does, unfortunately, take a toll on how you manage your emotions. Your brain physically changes, and your nervous system remains constantly dysregulated. Throughout my research, I have discovered that narcissistic abuse inflames and swells the amygdala and increases cortisol levels, leading sufferers to struggle to control their anxiety and anger. This is known as reactive anger. This explains so much about the deep-seated rage I felt for years and years.

These findings also mean that a target may be easily angered and may project their unconscious pain onto those they love and care about. This is what makes it so easy for the narcissist and "flying monkey" to "set off" and turn the tables back onto the target, but this anger isn't the target's fault; it's involuntary. The body is built to protect itself, after all. When you experience anxiety, depression, anger, or disassociation, that's your intuition talking. Trust the feelings inside your body and listen closely. These are symptoms, and they're not to be ignored.

Narcissists hover and cause harm, havoc, chaos, and pain in the life of every target they have. Anyone who has been targeted in this kind of situation is a victim of abuse. This includes the "scapegoat", the "scapegoat's" spouse, the "scapegoat's" children, and the "flying monkey" that is used by the narcissist. Yet the family "scapegoat" is often convinced that the abuse they are receiving is appropriate—deserved, even. I'm here to unconvince you of that. To my fellow family scapegoats: I see you, I feel you, and I love you. You do not deserve to be traumatized over and over. Repeated abuse creates complex PTSD, and trauma is detrimental to the mind, body, and spirit. No one deserves to be treated this way.

Reckoning With Narcissism in Ourselves

It's important to look at the narcissistic traits within yourself if you are to end generational trauma and realign an entire generation. This is the work that puts you on your path to valor.

The word "narcissism" is thrown around a lot these days, and indeed, there are narcissistic characteristics in *all* of us. So you can better identify these traits in yourself, let's examine many behaviors and signs of narcissism. What do these traits look like when they reside within yourself?

- Having very little compassion or empathy for others.
- Being unable to see others' perspectives.
- Belittling, criticizing, and judging others self-righteously.

- Having feelings of superiority and "all-knowing."
- Having the need for constant control.
- Lack of responsibility; blaming and deflecting.
- Selfishness and self-involvement. You cannot see how your actions/words hurt others.
- Lack of emotional maturity and intelligence.
- Taking credit for everything that goes well and rejecting the notion that you could be responsible for anything bad that occurs.
- "Testing" others, to push them to their breaking point.
- Constantly talking about the doom and gloom of the world and others; shifting your anxiety onto others.
- Lack of integrity, authenticity, and honesty.
- Inability to be truly vulnerable or using others' vulnerability against them.
- Inability to work as a team and to communicate for the common good.
- Displaying acts of kindness but with an ulterior motive, to get something in return.

This list isn't exhaustive. However, it hits many points. Feel free to add more to the list, should you be able to identify any more traits.

Building awareness of your own narcissistic traits and how you, as an individual, are contributing to your relationships is so important if you want your relationships to not only survive, but thrive.

Circle any traits in the previous list that you may have identified within yourself, or just make a mental note of them. I know this can be difficult, but it truly is necessary if you are going to take ultimate responsibility for yourself. You can't change without first building awareness of *what* needs to change. Besides, there is no shame in the game. This is part of you learning who you are, getting real, and being vulnerable. When you live with integrity, you become able to take ownership and make the shifts necessary to not only repair your relationships with others, but with yourself. To break free from generational trauma, you must learn to reparent yourself. This takes tremendous courage and bravery and is where your valor is.

Your ego will protect these "shadow" parts of you. Many people spend a lifetime not truly self-reflecting, as they are more comfortable with playing the "victim" role. But playing the victim isn't truly living.

I would also like to compassionately point out the fact that if you currently reject the idea that there could even be a smidge of narcissism living inside you, that in itself might indicate that you do have narcissist traits. I mean, are you Mother Teresa? No, you are not. Slightly harsh, but we are being honest here, aren't we?

Many of us Gen Xers were offered very little compassion and empathy as kids. We were raised with the "pull yourself up from your bootstraps" and "get over it and suck it up" attitude. We were taught that people who talk about their feelings are soft and weak; that we should never let them see us sweat, and most definitely not cry. You need to ask yourself (as a fellow Gen Xer) if you are projecting this lack of compassion and empathy you received as a child onto yourself, your partner, and the next generation. If the answer is "yes," bring compassion and empathy back to your heart, not only for the sake of yourself, but for the sake of everyone around you.

Start with yourself first.

Do you feel the need to control everything in your life (including those you've surrounded yourself with) because your home was so out of control or unpredictable when you were a child (and maybe even when you were a younger adult)? Are you now compensating for those feelings of powerlessness you had by being controlling and manipulative? Do you feel like the only sanctuary where you now find control and safety is behind your own closed doors? If the answer is "yes," open your door, step outside, and breathe in everything this beautiful universe has to offer you. Take responsibility for your life and your actions.

Many people categorize those with narcissistic behaviors as people who need to be cast aside by society, but I have deep compassion for the fact that such behaviors are developed over time as a means to gain love and control. The narcissist has been separated from their positive core human characteristics, such as unconditional love, empathy, and compassion, and that is a tragic thing. Let's reverse this damage by doing the work.

Healing From Narcissism

Whether you're being targeted by a narcissist or are realizing you yourself have narcissistic tendencies, having integrity and honesty is the best way to love and honor yourself first. You can bring your nervous system back online and you can bring your body back to a feeling of safety and calm through the correct use of boundaries. My courses focus on the steps you can take to bring your mind, body, and spirit into calm and peace and to release anger and anxiety after narcissistic abuse (and abuse in general). My clients have reported great appreciation for the tools I've provided; they have given them great results in their personal growth.

Remember that boundaries are for you. If there's someone in your life who continually crosses them, that is about them, not you. You deserve a life full of peace and harmony so you can thrive and become the best version of yourself, and it is extremely difficult to do this when someone is creating constant chaos in your life. When someone shows you repeatedly who they are, believe them and implement boundaries, no matter how scary it may be.

I also want you to remember that it's ultimately the narcissist's responsibility to heal. This means that if *you* are the narcissist in the equation, you need to dedicate yourself to self-healing. Also do not shame yourself for any coping mechanisms you may have acquired because of your abuse. Start trusting yourself and those who truly support your growth.

Going "no contact" is usually the first step to recovery. I cut off all communication with my mother and sisters because I was being gang bullied. I also hired a family law attorney to write a letter to my mother telling her to cease all attempts at communication with me, my husband, and my daughters. Such attempts at contact had left me full of anxiety and anger for too long, making healing even more difficult. Take this step, and you will already be halfway there.

You have the power to choose who's in your life and who isn't. Period. Take your power back. In fact, grab it and run with it. Implement the tips I've given you for regulating your nervous system and remember that if you have a lot of rage inside, this is normal, and I can help bring you back to peace. Journaling and respecting the pause (which I spoke to you about in Chapter 1 and offer a free course on) are fantastic ways to begin.

Another word of advice before we move on: if you have someone in your life that you know has been repeatedly lying about or talking poorly of others, do not think for an instant they won't do the same to you. They will, one hundred percent of the time. If your gut is telling you there is something off, trust this and do not put yourself in a situation where you are alone with a person like this (this allows for easy deniability of what was said). I started bringing my husband with me to nearly every face-to-face encounter I had with my mother as I became more and more aware of her false accusations and lies, and if you do the same with any narcissists in your life, this will also give you the validation that what you are feeling and seeing is real.

I would also like to mention here that as you progress on your healing journey, you may develop a healthy amount of confidence, self-belief, and self-love that might be misconstrued by others as negative narcissistic traits. Don't let this get you down. You are worthy of having these characteristics. It's your birthright! You are worthy of the strength and courage that it takes to heal, no matter what anyone else says about it.

When you treat yourself better, you allow yourself to show up better for your kids and your partner. Follow your intuition and your heart. If your own health and wellbeing aren't motivation enough, consider the fact that a dysfunctional family unit will lead to further dysfunction in your own children's lives if it is left unresolved, and in *their* children's lives. Investing in yourself is something to take great pride in, and modeling this in front of your children speaks volumes (and will convert into them also living a healthier life, with a deeper understanding of self-love and self-care).

If you're stuck in patterns with your parents and siblings that are damaging and that throw you into loops of arguing or long periods of silence, a resolution and change of behavior can help to break that loop. First, though, you need to absorb the fact that *healing starts with you* and that you owe no one an explanation for it. Self-loyalty must come first. If you're told you're being selfish, that's okay: be selfish with your healing! Giving your power to someone else in exchange for love and approval isn't a recipe for growth; it's a recipe for staying *exactly the same*. Calmly standing in your own power, on the other hand, is a recipe for growth. This means understanding that your parents did the best they could due to their own beliefs and childhood trauma (and having compassion for them), and also leading and reparenting yourself in alignment with the new life you know you truly deserve and want. Let their paradigms fall away to allow room for the new beliefs and new growth needed within you. If necessary, seek professional help from a coach or mentor who deeply understands the mind of a narcissist (if this is a situation you're dealing with right now).

To conclude this chapter: to all the black sheep/scapegoats out there, please know what a gift you are to your family lineage. Being abandoned or going "no contact" can feel incredibly lonely, but you can take comfort in the knowledge that thousands of your ancestors have been waiting for you and are cheering you on in your healing journey. You are shrouded in divine protection by a much higher power which has assigned you the task of being the one to break the dysfunction in your family line. Your strength and power to stand up against a family system meant to destroy and break you comes only from the rising phoenix within you.

While it may not feel like it, it is a golden, once-in-a-lifetime opportunity to grow a new healthy branch on your family tree; to be the first emotionally healthy person in your bloodline. Your ability to intuitively feel and identify the injustices cast upon you and others is what makes you so incredibly unique. This uniqueness is what your family line has been waiting for. You've taken the courageous path into the unknown to not only be true to your heart, but to also do the work that will affect and influence generations to come.

This is your legacy—a legacy that can never be taken from you, and an incredibly powerful legacy to leave. It's your legacy of beauty, grace, and valor, and it will live on in eternity.

5

Marriage and Partnerships

EMINEM (A GEN XER) IDENTIFIES the fact that he and his partner say and do things that they don't mean in his song *Love the Way You Lie*. He and his partner are repeating the same patterns and routines, and he says that his partner's temper is just as bad as his. He also thinks his partner is blinded to what love really is.

As someone who is also a Gen Xer, ask yourself, how do you envision a typical romantic relationship looking? Do you imagine something very similar to what you saw when you were growing up, between your parents? Are you normalizing the same patterns and routines they did? Have you been blinded to what mature, unconditional love looks like?

Many of us come to understand what love "is" or "should be" through our subconscious conditioning — that is, through what we observe from our parents and their relationships, society, cultural norms, social media, TV shows, and movies. In most cases, Gen Xers grew up thinking that love is "meant to be" an emotional rollercoaster, with huge highs and lows; that love means sticking by someone "no matter what." From being very young, we watched movies that conditioned us into believing that dysfunctional relationships are "just the way it is" and something to be normalized.

This dysfunction has been passed down from one generation to the next.

I remember hearing or reading somewhere that you don't get a medal for remaining in an unhappy, dysfunctional relationship for years on end, and this really resonated with me. After all, society still says that the longer you are married for, the more the relationship should be celebrated. In other words, twenty-five years, or fifty years, or a lifetime, of marriage—regardless of whether that's a *healthy* marriage—is to be celebrated.

I'm not encouraging you to abandon your relationship. What I am encouraging is for you to self-reflect and consider the role you play in your romantic relationship, and how your subconscious behavioral patterns affect that role. I am encouraging you to examine what perceptions of love have been passed down to you, so you can build awareness about your conditioning, and to build boundaries, so you can care for yourself, your partner, and your children better. I am encouraging you to swap your emotional rollercoaster ride for an even, steady track so you can create peace, harmony, and balance.

While the attraction you feel at the beginning of a relationship may feel intoxicating, people's masks eventually fall away, and shit gets real. At this point, your subconscious conditioning surrounding what a relationship or marriage is "supposed to look like" will take over—*if* you're not aware of your subconscious conditioning.

The love we feel at the beginning of a relationship is what we tend to hold onto. Many of us Gen Xers believe that it's healthy to accept poor treatment from our partners, or for us to "dish it out" because "that's what love is." This is untrue and unhealthy, and such beliefs and behaviors can be transformed, for the better.

A few years ago, a certain subconscious behavioral pattern of mine caused my husband pain, which made him emotionally withdraw. We went for a walk together in a park to discuss this problem (which, by the way, is therapeutic all in itself), and toward the end of the conversation, he jokingly said to me, "People really need to enter relationships with a script about their childhood and adult traumas." We both laughed. The idea was genius and so on point. Learning about yourself, your core wounding, your conditioning, and your own subconscious behavioral patterns will bring this much-needed clarity about why you behave the way you do in your intimate partnerships.

Many of us bond unconsciously through trauma, whether our childhood trauma or our traumas from past relationships. Consider whether you and your partner have similar core woundings. I'm not a gambling type of person, but I would bet that at least one (if not more) of your core woundings are similar. You may not have faced the exact same circumstances, but there may be some overlaps in the overarching themes of your traumas. These could be having a parent in childhood who denied your reality, did not see or hear you, vicariously lived through you or attempted to mold and shape you, did not model boundaries, was overly focused on appearances, or could not regulate their emotions (thereby unconsciously creating feelings of "I'm not good enough" and "I'm unworthy of love"). Your shared traumas could also be some form of childhood abandonment, physical abuse, emotional abuse, or physical or emotional neglect.

If you look deeply enough into your respective childhoods, you'll be able to find this similarity — I guarantee. Again, there will be variations in the exact story of how the trauma came to be, but the theme is what's relevant here.

Trauma bonds are normal, and they don't mean you should abandon the relationship altogether, or that your bond hasn't also been formed through mutual affection and compatibility. What they do mean is, you should look at how the trauma bond and codependency affects the health of your relationship and your attachment style.

When you have chosen your partners, chances are that you have selected people who felt like home in terms of their emotional maturity and emotional intelligence, in relation to your parents, your childhood, and what you witnessed during your formative years. In doing so, you could be repeating many unhealthy behavioral patterns that are very damaging to a relationship. Love is not pain, yet as a kid, you may have believed that your parents loved you even though they were inflicting physical or emotional pain on you. Because of this, you may still operate under the guise of "love" and "pain" being synonymous, or at least a package deal.

When you have failed relationships, one after another, there is one common denominator, and that is you. (I strongly suggest highlighting or circling that last sentence.) At some point, you must recognize the part you play in your relationships. What type of people are you attracting? Write down how closely they mirror your parents on an emotional maturity level. What are your patterns and relational routines that keep you repeating the same mistakes over and over and not learning from them? Think about this one deeply. Start taking ownership for the part you've played in your relationship history. Write these patterns down and be honest. Our partners are mirrors: they reflect back to us our unhealed wounding. For example, my father was extremely controlling, strict, violent, and overbearing, and my mother was emotionally immature, manipulative, and violent, too. I constantly lived in fear of both of my parents, yet I ended up choosing a partner like this (minus the violence), and thereby unconsciously set up the exact same relationship with that partner as the one I'd had with my parents. Conflict, to me, warned of violence and rage, so I learned to run away (flight), avoid, and disassociate to keep myself safe in my adult relationships. Even though there wasn't any violence, my body still detected danger all the time, because it associated conflict with violence. The body remembers, and my feelings were very natural, given the violent attacks I'd witnessed and endured in my childhood and throughout my adulthood.

The body will take the route that it thinks it needs to in order to survive. It is wired and programmed to keep itself safe at all costs, and this wiring (as we established earlier) is developed at a very young age. So, in adulthood, "flight" was a go-to nervous system response for me. Alternatively, if I wasn't fleeing the scene of a conflict, I was staying and attempting to fight it out. There really was no in between for me. Alcohol was also usually in the picture, so I could cope with the fear and anxiety my body felt while I was in these situations.

I share this so you can recognize and build awareness of your dysfunctional survival habits. I advise you to think on this topic in depth if you've ever been emotionally or physically abused (especially in your childhood). How could you be recreating the same patterns and routines in your current relationships that started long ago for survival?

My own infidelity was the cause and destruction of one of my marriages. I was unconsciously deeply traumatized, as most individuals who cheat are. This isn't an excuse, mind. I needed to go super-deep to figure out why I would treat someone like this; to understand why I would sabotage my own marriage. There is a lesson there, and blaming the other person in the relationship and leaving your survival patterns unchecked will have you repeating the same scenario repeatedly. Remember, you are the common denominator in your relationships, and you will unconsciously recreate scenarios from your childhood in your relationships — scenarios that keep you feeling unloved and abandoned — if you don't analyze your behavioral patterns.

This is deep work. Understanding your own flaws in your emotional intelligence and maturity is so valuable. Many of us stop emotionally maturing at a very young age, and we often mirror the emotional immaturity of our caregivers. Emotional maturity requires a great deal of emotional intelligence.

Emotional Maturity Within a Relationship

Emotional maturity can be defined as "knowing and modeling how to navigate through conversations with empathy and compassion for others, while also holding onto your own integrity." It means calmly understanding the views and perspectives of others, actively listening to them, and giving respect as you make a combined effort to resolve a conflict.

Emotional maturity *is*:

- Having healthy boundaries.
- Taking care of your nervous system.
- Taking care of your body and having healthy eating habits.
- Having a life of your own outside your marriage or kids' lives.
- Having productive, emotionally regulated conversations.
- Feeling secure in feeling all your emotions, without projecting them onto others.
- Holding space for yourself and others when you're/they're dysregulated by stating, "I need ten minutes to take a break from this," and returning when self-regulation has settled back in.
- Communicating your needs calmly and in the way that makes you feel loved and safe.
- Meeting your own needs.
- Recognizing that you are ultimately responsible for your own

behaviors and happiness.

- Discussing problems with an end goal of resolving them, in a way that only focuses on the current issue.
- Viewing triggers as opportunities for growth and taking responsibility for them.
- Listening to understand, not to respond.
- Truly leaning in to hear and feel what the other person is saying (this requires "respecting the pause").
- Understanding that there are multiple realities and perspectives in every situation.
- Feeling comfortable with being emotionally vulnerable and open.
- Having self-awareness regarding your patterns and conditioning and seeking to grow.
- Forgiving yourself and others easily.
- Not judging yourself and others.
- Apologizing with heartfelt compassion and empathy, and seeking to change the behavior.
- Validating others and their feelings.
- Understanding that relationships are a safe space for growth.

Emotional maturity is *not*:
- Yelling in attempt to control or intimidate.
- Blaming others for your behavior.
- Manipulating through guilt and shame.
- People-pleasing/self-betrayal.
- Playing the victim.
- Reminding your partner or kids of "all that you've done for them."
- Black-and-white thinking.
- Having no boundaries.

- Being "out to win" during a conflict and keeping the score from previous unresolved issues.
- Using the past as a weapon to divert from the current topic.
- Talking over others.
- Hurting someone's feelings and then telling them they are "too sensitive" or that you were joking.
- Expecting partners or others to know how you are feeling without you communicating directly.
- Expecting others to make you happy or to please you.
- Self-abandonment/-betrayal to keep the peace.
- Gossiping, chronic involvement in drama, making demeaning remarks, and eye-rolling.
- Using someone's vulnerability against them later, during a conflict.
- Denying someone's feelings or telling them to "suck it up" or that it's "no big deal."
- Lacking self-awareness about your patterns and conditioning.
- Projecting past relationship patterns/hurts onto the current relationship.
- Being unable to compassionately apologize (or not apologizing at all).
- Consistently threatening a divorce/breakup as a means to manipulate.
- Suppressing emotions with unhealthy sources.
- Being passive-aggressive and using silent treatment.

There are many other examples of emotional maturity and immaturity. Feel free to add some of your own to the lists and circle the ones that may apply to you.

Remember that your healing journey is yours, and while my

suggestion is for you to take the time to recognize the emotionally mature and immature parts of yourself, it's inevitable that you will also recognize such traits in others. Focus on yourself, though, instead of self-righteously diagnosing other people. We're focused on *your* valor right now, not anyone else's — which also means we need to focus on just *your* strengths and weaknesses.

Lies

Honesty is absolutely foundational to the conversation of emotional maturity within intimate relationships. They can be a real make-or-break factor.

We start telling lies as children, for multiple reasons, including to protect ourselves or get a need met. This process is nearly unconscious when you're a small child. In our teenage years, it becomes more conscious but still common practice.

How many times did you lie or twist the truth to avoid "punishment" in childhood? Similarly, how many times have you unconsciously lied in your partnership so you could avoid dealing with the consequences of your actions? How many times have you hidden something from your partner and told yourself a story justifying why you "needed" to do so?

When you lie, this is you trying to avoid getting into "trouble." In other words, you are trying to avoid being shamed, guilted, or punished, much like in your childhood.

This strategy for conflict avoidance doesn't work if you want to step into your valor and approach your relationships with emotional maturity. Stepping into your valor means living with integrity. It means saying and owning your truth, no matter how uncomfortable it makes someone else.

If we shouldn't lie, how *should* we navigate conflict?

Navigating Conflict

Conflicts are merely opportunities for growth, *if* all parties involved have a regulated nervous system, understand that problems are inevitable and can be dealt with, and have the goal of approaching the entire situation with emotional maturity. Let's explore how we can foster these qualities in your approach to conflict management.

If conflict meant emotional dysregulation in your childhood, you most likely don't like the word, and chances are, you have a similar way of managing it as one (or both) of your parents/caregivers. This might involve shutting down for long periods of time (i.e., silent treatment), walking on eggshells, screaming or yelling, or gaslighting.

Emotional maturity will allow you to embrace the idea that a problem within a relationship is an opportunity for each member to be heard, seen, and unconditionally loved, rather than something to be avoided and that leads to the slow, steady buildup of silence or high emotions (ultimately leading to a breakdown within the relationship).

Moving On From Conflicts

If you notice that you're consistently bringing up or feeling connected to things that happened in the past, this is the opposite of emotional maturity, and you need to make the conscious decision to either address them or let them go. If a genuine apology was made at the time and there was an agreement to move on, then march forward and do not bring it up again (so long as the person's apologetic words are reflected in their behavior).

Doing this is a triumph. It is you letting your ego and body know that you are safe in the present moment and that the past needs to be left where it is; that you are capable of navigating conflicts, regardless of how you've navigated them in the past; that you are smart and beautiful; that you are deserving of love and are able to freely give love even during times of conflict.

More Boundaries

Again, conflicts are there to help relationships move forward and grow. So they feel easier to manage, my suggestion is for you to have a set of conflict boundaries for yourself and your partner. What does that mean? It means literally making a list of the ways in which you currently navigate conflicts and identifying what parts of this list are no longer serving you and your partner.

At the top of the list, write, "Conflicts are an opportunity for growth and for everyone to be heard, seen, and loved." Then, write down how you want to show up during a conflict. Imagine yourself as someone who is soft, kind, open, and vulnerable.

It is important to note that some conflict strategies that resonate with you may not resonate with your partner. It is critical to respect and honor yourself and your partner as autonomous, unique beings. Focus on the beautiful aspects of your partner and the good that they bring into your life. Do they support you and your growth? I hope so! Do you believe people can change their behavior? Most human beings absolutely can, so long as they still have unconditional love and patience for themselves and their partner under their belt. Your approach to conflict navigation should be underpinned by appreciation and gratitude for all the amazing things in life, within yourself and your partner.

Also remember that emotional maturity means taking ultimate responsibility for the mistakes you've made and not just pointing out your partner's mistakes and their emotional immaturity. It requires you to take that first step. Give unconditional love to yourself and your partner, while creating boundaries.

Your new boundaries can include strategies for regulating your nervous system during and after a conflict. Hopefully you, as a couple, will usually be able to "respect the pause" before a conflict escalates, but sometimes, this doesn't happen, and we need healthy ways to regulate ourselves mid-conflict. Asking for time out or space away for ten to twenty minutes can allow your nervous system to calm, as can heartfelt apologies, touching your partner's hand or shoulder, hugging, or looking your partner in the eyes when an apology is given.

Crying

Go ahead and cry if you need to while navigating conflict. Yes, really! Many of us Gen Xers have a hard time crying and being vulnerable, because we've been conditioned to not cry. Words like, "If you don't stop crying, I'll give you something to cry about," have likely been programmed into your subconscious. Perhaps you were told that crying means showing weakness. Maybe whenever you begin to cry, you apologize for it. (Do not apologize for crying. Ever.)

Allowing yourself to cry shows you are a human with feelings, and it allows you to release the stress, hurt, and pain that you are pushing down deep. Besides, when you stop yourself from crying, you keep the nervous system in a dysregulated state. Crying helps to reset your nervous system.

What I find interesting in working with clients is, many of us have such a difficult time crying and letting our emotions out. Even more interesting is the fact that some people are angered by someone else's crying. Perhaps they had a parent who was angered when they cried.

Are you projecting this kind of conditioning onto yourself or your partner?

Either way, crying is the body's natural response to certain feelings. You need to honor this process, in yourself and others, if you are to exercise emotional maturity and step into your valor.

Apologizing

Prince's *Purple Rain* resonates when it comes to apologies and making changes to relationships. So many of us Gen Xers have trouble with making true, heartfelt apologies and changes within ourselves and our relationships. In general, the majority of us don't mean to cause pain and heartache to those we love the most.

All apologies you give need to be sincere, with no use of the word "but," no overexplaining, and no blaming or shaming. Just plain and simple, "I'm sorry I hurt you."

Once you have apologized, ask your partner how you can help to repair and validate their feelings, even if your thoughts and opinions on the situation do not align. You are not here to tell people how they should or should not feel. Instead, learn how those you love prefer to be treated and what their boundaries are (and what will happen if the boundaries are crossed), and communicate to them what your boundaries are. For example, if your partner begins screaming, let them know that you will leave the room and come back to repair the conflict when they are calm. Do the same for yourself, too: if you feel emotions bubbling up, take a break. This is how you show love and respect for others and yourself.

Again, conflict doesn't need to be treated like an alarm going off in a house on fire. Slow down, pause, give thoughtful responses, and listen with love, compassion, and empathy.

Do you struggle to apologize? If so, you probably lived with a lot of shame as a child. Such Gen Xers report that apologizing, for them, elicits feelings of deep shame that make it extremely difficult to communicate any remorse. If this is the case for you, I suggest writing the apology down in a letter. Ask to read the letter to your partner out loud and let yourself cry.

You may also struggle to accept heartfelt apologies (not just give them). Consider, when someone gives you a heartfelt apology, are you able to truly, one hundred percent accept the apology, let it go, and never bring it up again? Many Gen Xers find they cannot accept an apology and need multiple apologies over long periods of time in order to move on. In this situation, it is likely that the conflict in question unconsciously retriggered an underlying unhealed core wound that had nothing to do with their partner.

An important note: I'm not talking about being unable to forgive repeated abuse here. I'm talking about day-to-day conflicts and apologies. We all make big and small mistakes every day (because we are human). These are the kinds of conflicts I'm talking about.

Behavioral Patterns versus Isolated Incidents

There's a difference between behavioral patterns that occur over a long period of time and an isolated incident. I call an isolated incident a "one off." An isolated incident occurs when you're going along, everything appearing to be fine in the relationship, but there's an underlying, slow buildup of hurt and resentment, and one or both of you feel unheard or unseen. Then, when there's a "one off," it's like an explosion—like releasing a valve that's been under pressure over an extended period—and the individual just snaps and vomits verbal diarrhea everywhere.

Perhaps they even become violent by stomping around the house, slamming doors, throwing things, and yelling at everyone. This is usually uncharacteristic of the individual.

Why does this happen? Because the individual is suppressing their wants and needs (and likely betraying themselves) to keep the peace.

To avoid falling down this slippery slope, you must be brave enough to have hard conversations, even if that means disappointing someone else. You must get into the habit of holding true to what matters to you and what allows you to feel safe within your relationship.

Identify what in your relationship currently causes you to feel (emotionally) unsafe. Write it in the blank space on this page. Then, write what would make you feel safe. This will help you to identify where boundaries are needed.

If your boundaries are invalidated and ignored by your partner (or anyone else in your life, for that matter), then you know it's time to shift your own behavior and take responsibility for what you are allowing in your life. You may need to end the relationship if your partner shows they are really unwilling to respect your boundaries.

We are adults, and adults can handle disappointment. What most can't handle is unconscious self-betrayal. This in mind, are you repeatedly ignoring your wants and needs? Do you have a *partner* who ignores your wants and needs, even after you've communicated them multiple times? Regularly communicating your boundaries and wants and needs, even if they're as simple as needing a clean, uncluttered space (as one of my clients shared), is a healthy way to navigate through the big and small things. Having equal respect for one another's hearts and mental and physical wellbeing is paramount to creating change within our relationships.

You can choose to cultivate what you want in your relationship by opening your heart and having deep, vulnerable conversations. This starts with you.

Attachment Styles

There are four core attachment styles: secure, anxious, avoidant, and disorganized. You will need to understand these if you are to navigate your intimate relationships with self-awareness and a regulated nervous system.

Typically, an intimate relationship involves someone who is aggressive and someone who is passive-aggressive; someone who wants to "fight it out" when they become dysregulated and someone who dissociates and shuts down, with long periods of silence. One party wants to resolve the situation and is exhaustively chasing the other, who has emotionally shut down and is pulling away. This ignites a core wound in the pursuer, who doesn't feel seen or heard.

This is an example of the relationship dynamics between an anxious and an avoidant attachment style.

Alternatively, both parties may emotionally shut down and no longer try to find a resolution when they become dysregulated. They form no agreement to revisit the issue and instead just brush it under the carpet. This leads to underlying hurt and resentment and the pattern repeating itself over and over. This is what happens in a relationship with two avoidants.

Identifying your attachment style will help you to communicate the ways in which your partner can help you to feel loved and understood. Let's dive into each attachment style so you can identify yours.

Anxious:

- Desires consistent reassurance.
- Is hyperaware of shifts in people's moods and behaviors.
- Becomes anxious or emotionally overwhelmed during conflicts, and wants to quickly resolve it to ease their discomfort.
- Needs a lot of physical contact and frequent communication through calls or texts.
- Can be viewed as "needy" or "clingy."
- Can struggle with setting boundaries and respecting others' boundaries.
- Has a strong fear of abandonment and rejection.

Avoidant:

- Has difficulty sharing feelings and being vulnerable.
- Shuts down when they sense shifts in people's moods and behaviors.
- Attempts to avoid a conflict by changing the subject, withdrawing, or going silent.
- Becomes uncomfortable when there is too much physical contact and closeness.
- Can be cold and distant.
- Has stiff boundaries and expectations of others.
- Has a strong fear of abandonment and rejection.

Disorganized:

- Struggles knowing what they want or need.
- Is unsure of people's intentions and shifts in moods and behavior.
- Can be viewed as chaotic and unpredictable during conflicts.
- Varies between needing a lot of contact and no contact.
- Is inconsistent with boundary-setting and respecting others'

boundaries.

- Has a strong fear of abandonment and rejection.

Secure:

- Openly and confidently expresses their wants and needs.
- Trusts that people usually have good intentions, but is not blind to red flags.
- Understands that conflicts are inevitable and is able to navigate them in a calm, productive manner.
- Understands the importance of balance between alone time and closeness.
- Consistently shows up in relationships as a cooperative and flexible participant.
- Copes with occasional fear of abandonment and rejection appropriately.

Your attachment style is not fixed for life, nor should it be.

A particular attachment style's characteristics may resonate with you in some ways, but not others. Either way, I want you to become aware of your attachment style(s) and behaviors and acknowledge where you may fall, so you can begin working toward building a secure attachment style with yourself and others. This is taking responsibility for yourself and making the changes needed to have a healthier and well-balanced relationship with everyone in your life.

Love Languages

You singlehandedly have the ability to create excitement and fun in your partnership, and this becomes especially achievable when you intentionally take the time to cultivate deeper intimacy and love, have open, vulnerable conversations about sex (and spice things up in the bedroom!), schedule time together to do things that bring you both joy, happiness, and peace, don't betray yourself or pretend to like what you think your partner wants you to like when it comes to having fun, be true to yourself, and venture to learn and try new and different things together. All of this starts with you understanding your own attachment style and shifting into building a more secure attachment with yourself.

Expecting your partner to know what you want and need is emotionally immature and naïve. Do *you* even know what you need and want in a relationship in order to feel loved? Think about it.

I want you to write down what makes you feel loved, right now. Get a Post-It or write directly in the margins of this book. Is it handholding? Daily kisses? Long hugs? Sitting next to your partner on the couch? Being given gratitude? Being given love notes? A meal being prepared for you by your partner?

So many of us give love to our partners from a space of how *we* like to feel love, rather than how *they* do. Ask yourself if you are loving your partner from a space of how *they* feel appreciation and love. Open a conversation about it. Make a list with them.

Conversations about love languages remind me of the song *Escape (The Piña Colada Song)* by Rupert Holmes. This song tells a story of how a wife puts an ad in the paper looking for someone who likes the same things as her, and her husband, not knowing that the ad was posted by his wife, answers it. They agree to meet up and are surprised it's each other, because they never knew what the other actually liked.

When you don't communicate how you like to be loved, your relationship can grow stale and lead to you falling into the same old routines. Learning and communicating your love language can be beautiful and help you to build deeper intimacy, even if you've been in a relationship for a long period of time. This is healthy to frequently bring up when you're discussing day-to-day acts of love, dates, vacations, and what goes on in the bedroom with your partner.

Note that how you like to be loved will change and evolve over time (as it should), so this is also a conversation that will sometimes need to be revisited.

Unconditional Love versus Conditional Love

UNCONDITIONAL LOVE	CONDITIONAL LOVE
Accepting someone for who they are.	Shaming a person for who they are and attempting to change them through threats, tough love, and manipulation.
Loving someone without limitations or conditions.	Loving someone under conditions and set limitations.
Loving someone even when a conflict arises and being dedicated to resolving the conflict.	Turning your love "on and off," or withholding it, in the face of conflict.
Loving someone from a space of conscious self-awareness.	Loving someone from an ego-based and self-serving space.
Being unjudgmental toward the people you love.	Being judgmental toward the people you love.

What's the difference between unconditional love and conditional love? The previous chart demonstrates these differences.

Think about the type of love you are giving and receiving. Is it conditional love? This is where you don't accept someone for who they are, attempt to manipulate them or withhold love and affection to get them to be who you want them to be, or withhold sex or affection without clearly, honestly, and directly expressing your wants, needs, and issues.

Do you have a "tit for tat," transactional relationship ("You do this for me and then I'll do this for you")? Do you make others earn your love before you offer love in return? Do you lack trust in your partner because your trust was broken early in your childhood or in a previous relationship? Are you constantly judging or criticizing your partner? Do you need your partner to be perfect all the time? Do you need to be right and in control of everything all the time?

Underline or highlight the conditional love you might be giving and receiving.

Conditional love involves power imbalances. Maybe there are parent-child dynamics between you and your partner, and this means you don't both work on the same team for the same general desired outcomes. Have you unconsciously set up this scenario? Are you unconsciously sabotaging your relationship because deep down, you feel unlovable and fear that you will be abandoned (like you perhaps were in childhood or in a previous relationship)? Are you claiming to not "need" help or support? Is there a wounded ego and power struggle constantly at play in your relationship? Do you have control issues? Do you criticize your partner and boss them around because deep inside, you feel out of control? Do you keep the score, deflect, and bring up the past to divert from acknowledging your feelings (this is also known as gaslighting)? Be honest! Be vulnerable, Gen X!

Conditional love will wear at a relationship and cause a lot of resentment and pain, especially during hard times.

Unconditional love, on the other hand, means always honoring one another, even during conflict and the darkest and hardest times. It means believing that the situation is temporary and will get better.

Unconditional love is pure and beautiful, like a newborn baby. Unconditional love means loving a person from the depths of your soul in a way that is divine, unbridled, infinite, whole, blissful, healthy, and multidimensional.

Unconditional love can exist between a parent and a child, siblings, lovers, friends, and even pets. It's an abundant kind of love. There is plenty of it to go around, for each type of relationship in your life to flourish.

Emotional maturity and unconditional love, in combination, means listening to your partner and validating their feelings while focusing on the present moment and resolving to move forward. It means showing daily gratitude and love for your partner and celebrating them for the small moments of success (not just the big moments or on special occasions). It means not withholding love, even during conflicts, and holding space for yourself, so you can take the time to feel your feelings.

Yep! Feel your feelings.

The goal here isn't to be perfect or to have the perfect relationship. Life is messy. The goal is to have healthy loving relationships, and to realize that you are both human and will fuck up from time to time as you continue to grow and to learn from one another with an open heart. Love is beautiful when you give and receive from a place that is authentic, real, and raw. That's the really good stuff.

Should you wish to dig deeper into yourself and repair your partnerships even further, head to www.deniseconde.com for additional resources. You will absolutely find the support and guidance you need there.

6

Parenting from the Subconscious

AS WHITNEY HOUSTON ALLUDES TO in *Greatest Love of All*, learning to love yourself is the greatest act of love you could give to your children. As a parent, you must look at how you are contributing to your kids' emotional wellbeing through this lens: are you loving yourself? Do you see the beauty that you see in your child, in yourself? Once you heal and love yourself, you will be able to show up as a better parent for your children.

The outdated sentiment that you're the parent and that the child should do as they're told and respect you needs to be discarded, as does the idea that "children are to be seen and not heard" (which was possibly projected onto you). Respect is not earned; it's automatic, by virtue of you just being born and on this earth. The same applies for your children. You should therefore meet your children exactly where they are at in their development and honor each stage of their life.

Research shows that the brain becomes fully developed around the age of twenty-five. The system we've been raised in says that you're a legal adult when you're eighteen, but what is poorly reflected in the current body of research is the full picture of how long it actually takes for the brain to fully develop and to gain emotional maturity and intelligence. So, maybe you were kicked to the proverbial curb at the age of eighteen, but that doesn't mean you should do the same to your kids. Every human being, no matter what their age, deserves unconditional love and to feel heard, seen, and validated, so minimizing your child's reality is just harmful.

Something that I find quite interesting is the fact that kids with Gen X parents are generally *much* more attuned to their emotional wellbeing and what they will and will not stand for compared to Gen Xers themselves. They talk about their feelings, as opposed to Gen Xers, who were shamed for having feelings and told to suppress them because speaking up or "talking back" was viewed as a sign of disrespect. Kids nowadays know that they aren't being disrespectful or talking back when they do this, but that they are expressing their needs and wants and deserve to be heard and validated.

We now know that the tone in which something is said matters, and that you can project your unresolved trauma and core wounding onto your kids through that alone. There is now so much more information, proof, and neuroscience available to us that can aid us in healing ourselves and our relationships, so there's no excuse to not endeavor to improve in this area.

After one specific fit of unconscious anger toward my daughters, I remember thinking to myself that they were lucky that I hadn't become physically violent with them, like my parents had to me, and that they "had it so much better" than I'd had and "needed to toughen up." It was a major reality check for me when I reflected on this line of thinking. Screaming and yelling is emotional violence and is just as damaging as physical violence on a developing child's nervous system and self-worth.

Clearly, that line of thought, my mindset, and the lack of compassion and empathy offered to me as a child and an adult was being projected by me onto my daughters.

Kids need to feel consistently safe and to be able to trust the adults in their lives to be able to regulate their emotions. But the underlying unprocessed grief of my father's passing, the narcissistic abuse from my mother and oldest sibling, and the dysfunction within myself and my marriage all took a toll on my emotional wellness, leaving me easily triggered and angered.

This isn't an excuse — it's me taking responsibility for what I allowed in my life and therefore my daughters' lives — and I knew it was only damaging my relationship with them further.

While anger is an important emotion to feel (it teaches us where our boundaries are being crossed and where our needs are not being met), it's important to recognize where your anger is coming from, so you don't project it onto your children. My daughters have been the most important mirror of my own childhood and my past behavior, and for that, I am grateful. It can be extremely draining to fully acknowledge the impact and influence we have on our children, but ignoring it is *not* something I recommend. Remember, we are all imperfectly perfect, and we make mistakes so we can grow from them (yes, even into adulthood).

Are you ready to grow? If so, I can help you.

As you begin to understand yourself and your nervous system, subconscious, core woundings, and conditioning, it's important that you make shifts in your parenting so you can build stronger relationships with your children, no matter how old they are. This takes a great deal of courage and vulnerability, but you have this courage within you — the courage to love yourself and others, without harsh judgment and rejection entering the equation. A great deal of self-compassion is part of this journey.

The bottom line is, you were given a toolbox for parenting from your parents/caregivers, and while I'm hopeful that there's some good stuff in your toolbox, it's important for you to become aware of some of the shitty stuff in it that you may have unconsciously projected onto your kids. As previously discussed, when you don't actively care for yourself and your nervous system, you operate from survival mode and often revert to the subconscious parenting patterns you learned when you weren't consciously aware they were being formed.

There's always room for self-forgiveness and growth in your relationship with your kids, no matter how old you or they are.

Being a Safe Space

Part of being a conscious parent involves you taking your children's trials and tribulations seriously and being a safe space for them — the very same "safe space" that so many Gen Xers reject as a place for people that are "weak." This space signifies quite the opposite of weakness. So many of us Gen Xers never had a safe home to thrive in; a place where we could consistently rely on our caregivers to be calm, loving, and understanding. Many of us were even locked out of the house. You probably recall settling arguments through fist-fights or getting in someone's face. On the contrary to this, allowing your kids to grow means providing a space for them to make their own decisions and choices, and therefore their own mistakes.

We all learn best from experience rather than long lectures. Your kids will tune you out the longer you drone on and on about what they should and shouldn't do in life. Model critical thinking skills and staying calm during disagreements rather than shoving your thoughts and experiences down their throats. They must experience life on their own. It is, after all, their life, not yours. Modeling self-care, self-respect, and self-love will go a long way without you even saying a word.

In addition, there are lifechanging events that teenagers and young adults need to know about and receive your moral guidance on, such as drinking and driving, drug-use, and teenage pregnancy — things that can drastically alter their lives forever. Your kids won't seek your counsel on these topics if you haven't already created an established safe space for them. Educating your kids on these topics is very important, as is setting boundaries in your home in line with what you feel is and isn't appropriate. The facts are, kids are going to experiment if they have access to vapes, alcohol, and so on (I started using drugs and alcohol at the age of twelve, though that was obviously way too young for a brain that was still developing). Therefore, creating a safe space where kids can have these discussions and come to you when they become curious is super-important. It is also far more effective than just telling them not to do it, or having suspicions, catching them in the act, and punishing them.

This is not the same as *normalizing* such behaviors. It's about not being naïve and keeping a healthy dialogue about these topics going. For example, you can encourage your kids to have protected sex (rather than unprotected sex) by helping them through the process of finding safe birth control methods that suit them. Another example would be having discussions around masturbation and self-pleasure — specifically, about how it is healthy and how no one should ever feel ashamed for exploring their own body.

Being a Safe Space for Social Issues

Kids nowadays are covert in how they hurt and ostracize one another, so consistent and healthy parent-child communication is a must. This isn't to say bullying doesn't still exist; it's just largely done on social media and through the systematic ostracization of a member of a group, especially into the middle school and high school years. Kids still grapple for a position of power and control (just through much more psychological means), and this is usually led by a member of the group who controls who is and isn't in the group through lies and manipulation. Unlike in our day, this is done slowly and methodically: leaving the target on "Read"; kicking them out of a group chat; leaving them out of an in-person group discussion by turning their backs; saying hurtful remarks to dehumanize them; and so on and so forth. If any other group member speaks up or defends the target, they're kicked out of the group. (Has your kid experienced this? Ask them!) The remaining members meanwhile cower to the leader as a means of self-preservation, so they aren't outcasted, too. This is normalized, and the kids involved are left heartbroken.

It's cruel, and, as I know from a) being a parent who watched this happen at one time or another to both my daughters, b) being a teacher who saw this play out in her own classroom, and c) talking to parents about their children, it's repeated over and over. And to make matters worse (and what I'm getting at is), the parents of the kids who are still in the group brush it off because it's not happening to *their* kid, so they just ignore it or deny it — again, with words and actions they've been conditioned to use by their parents.

How do kids learn these tactics? Well, kids learn almost everything by watching their parents. Passive-aggressive traits are handed down from parents who consistently tell "white lies" as a means to get their needs met (professionally and personally); from parents who stonewall one another in a passive-aggressive way, normalize the behavior, and pretend everything's okay in the marriage when it's not; from parents who use manipulation to be "popular" and implicitly set out to "destroy" another person; from parents who are addicted to gossip and belittling and badmouthing others.

Children themselves are often also manipulated into doing things they don't want to by parents who are hyper-focused on "appearances" and how others view them. Parents who offer very little empathy and compassion toward their children and their reality produce people with low emotional intelligence and zero compassion for others.

All of this in mind, remember that the "drama" your kid is speaking of is real to them, and is extremely hurtful and damaging in a very concrete, valid way. Ignoring the problem at any age invalidates their reality and leads them to believe that no one is there to support them and help them through how they're feeling. They learn to invalidate themselves and their feelings and pretend that the situation doesn't bother them, when actually, it's tearing them apart inside.

What should you do instead? First, compassionately acknowledge your kid's pain and offer to help. Your kid might tell you that they don't want your help, but they do, trust me. They need an adult in their life to help them navigate their feelings; to stand up for what is in the best interests of their emotional wellbeing. Then, if necessary, bring it to the attention of the other parents or to the school. You can bet the other parents will deny the idea that their child could possibly do any harm to your child, so call for a face-to-face meeting with all relevant parents and kids present. Restorative justice is a very effective means of getting kids to talk through issues with very little interjection from the parents. This empowers kids to take turns talking so they can speak openly and honestly while the others listen intently to what is being said. Most schools are up to date on this practice, and it's often led by a school counselor.

Kids need to be taught to speak their truth about how they were hurt *while* also learning how to compassionately apologize, with no interruptions or use of the word "but."

I've used this method in situations involving my students and daughters, and it helped a great deal. This method is also great to use among your children and their siblings, to model how to navigate conflicts within the home and to give your children the right tools and language to take leadership in their lives (within their sibling relationships and also among their peers).

Yes, kids grow apart from their friends and change friend groups as they grow—we adults do the same thing—but there's a vast difference between growing into new friendships and ostracizing a member of a family or friend group through lies, gaslighting, and manipulation.

Parenting = Modeling

Note that when navigating parenthood, many subconscious means of parenting are not relevant or productive. Saying things like, "Back in my day, we did x," is nothing but unhelpful. It's no longer "back in your day." The past has passed. It's gone. Just like the eighties mullet, you need to let it go. Your job as a parent is not to control your kids' emotions or behaviors; your job is to control your *own* behaviors so you can model healthy emotions.

Whoa! What? Yes: control and model healthy behaviors, and your kids *will* model the same.

The truth is, our kids tend to test the very core of our woundings—they are little unfiltered truthtellers!—so if your child's wants and needs are triggering for you, perhaps investigate what core wounding this may be activating for you. Maybe you've asked your child to do something for the tenth time, and you now feel close to losing your shit because you are not feeling heard (and this reopens a wound from your childhood). In this situation, you will want to calmly get to the core of the problem and why the child might be intentionally ignoring your request. Kids struggle with transitioning from one thing to another at times, so expecting them to drop what they are doing immediately is unreasonable. Think about yourself and what it feels like when someone asks you to drop everything in an instant, when you are in the middle of something.

Try conveying directions, plans, and chores calmly, rather than yelling across the house. This is a very good habit to get into. Imagine if your boss yelled a bunch of instructions from another room. How well would you be able to remember and perform the tasks shouted at you? Think about it. Not very well, I bet. Your nervous system would likely shut down and disassociate from the yelling. Kids do the same thing.

It's normal for kids to want to do all the things their friends are doing, have relationships outside of the family home, and have their own autonomy, so if you have resentment toward your child because of this, you need to investigate that. If you've been parenting from your subconscious and taking away your kids' phones, or handing out consequence after consequence and ultimatums, and *nothing is changing their behavior*, they're clearly not feeling heard, validated, valued, or maybe even loved. Getting to the heart of the issue by listening to them, validating their feelings, acknowledging how that situation must be difficult for them, and offering help is much more effective.

Remember, kids *already* have a moral compass, and they usually know when they've made mistakes, so parent from a standpoint of "we all make mistakes, and mistakes are made to allow us to grow," rather than handing out a pile of consequences to fit the crime. Punishments build resentment, disconnection, guilt, and shame, and this turns children into people-pleasers — a.k.a., people who betray themselves in order to receive love. Next time you think, *A healthy amount of fear is a good thing*, or, *My kids need to respect me*, remember that *fear creates disconnection*. Plus, kids should never fear their parents. Think about when you lived in fear of your own parents and how that affected you. What did it do to your self-confidence and self-esteem? Do you walk around as an adult not feeling "good enough?" Answer that question and write it down in this book or on a separate piece of paper. Do you want your kids to not feel good enough? Of course not.

As a parent, it is your job to build a conscious life of safety and secure attachment for your child. If you want your kids to respect you, then you need to respect and love yourself and your partner. How do you respect yourself? You stop people-pleasing and betraying yourself to keep the peace (if you are), you take care of your body (through healthy eating, exercise, meditation, and so on), and you work to repair your marriage or partnership. Build a healthy life that your kids will reflect on and model in their own lives when they become an adult. If you want your kids to realize their dreams, you need to start realizing yours. If you want your kids to have healthy emotions, you need to start regulating yours and help them to navigate through theirs (rather than telling them to not feel the way they do, suppress their feelings, "start feeling differently," or go to their room). If you don't want your kids to lie, then you need to start telling the truth. (You also need to understand that kids lie to protect themselves from getting in "trouble" and to keep themselves safe. Lying doesn't have to mean the end of trust in your relationship with your kids; instead, it's an opportunity to understand why they felt they had to lie.)

Take ultimate responsibility for the life you've created for your children. Is it one of constant conflict and chaos? Discuss the nervous system and dysregulation with your children and invite them into the idea of regulating their nervous system. Explore the things that help to make them calm, such as the suggestions given in Chapter 1, and allow them to feel their emotions. Discuss the things that happen in the home that make your children feel scared or anxious.

Stop pretending that your kids don't feel what's happening in the home; they do! Your kids only feel safe when they live in a stable environment. If they think their home's stability is at risk, they will attempt to listen to everything they can to bring themselves back to safety and to be reassured their lives will not be upended. Kids can (and do) pick up on the vibe and energy in a household even before a word is said. Their nervous system is just like ours: it will go into "fight," "fight," "freeze," or "fawn" when it senses tension or conflict.

Our overarching message here is, your healing matters and is paramount to the lives of your children, regardless of their age. So, admit to the mistakes you've made. Apologize with compassion and honesty. You want them to grow and be responsible? Start growing within yourself and taking responsibility for the leadership in your home. Have you played favorites with one of your children? Have you called them names? If so, stop, own it, and apologize. Validate their feelings by saying, "I'm here and want you to feel validated." Tell them they are loved every day, no matter what. Let them know that their feelings matter and are important to you.

When you're having a sensitive conversation with your kids, repeat back to them what you're hearing. For example, "I'm hearing you are upset because x, y, and z." Say to them, "This must be hard for you. How can I help?" Tell them you honor their heart and that it is held by you. Be vulnerable and let them know that you realize you've made some mistakes and are working on making the relationship stronger.

You are the leader in their lives, so you are responsible for leading the way in healing your relationship with them. Your kids are not responsible for your lack of emotional regulation, nor are they responsible for controlling your behavior. You are.

Stop normalizing yelling and screaming to convey the importance of what you are trying to get at, or to pound something into your kid's head. Stop overcompensating for what you wanted and needed in your childhood and try to give your kids what they need from you. Start to observe where the roots of your anger lie. So many of us swear we'll never do to our children the things our parents did to us, yet we simultaneously convince ourselves that "we turned out okay" and that we can therefore repeat the same damaging parenting styles and behaviors over and over.

Your power and control weaken with every stage of your children's development, from the time you let go of their tiny little hands when they begin to walk on their own, to when they start developing friendships on their own, to when they get their license and gain their own independence, to when they start living on their own. This isn't a bad thing: you're here to guide your kids to their own independence, so they can think critically, make decisions for themselves, and create boundaries around how they want to be treated (even by you, the parent). Your child is not yours to keep forever. They are not a possession of yours, though your ego might tell you otherwise. Your children are not here to please you or to conform to your ways of life, but to create a life of their own that makes them happy and proud of themselves. Of course, your kids may *want* your approval, but should they betray themselves and the life they want in order to get it? No; it's their journey, not yours. You are here to offer guidance and unconditional love through every stage of their life. That's your job. Your children do not need to meet your expectations or gain your approval. Your kids need to set their own expectations and goals for their future, aided by your love and support.

Modeling Healthy Relationship Dynamics

Principally, you need to remember that people recreate the relationship dynamics that they witnessed in their childhoods. If your kids see or hear you discussing intimate matters about your spouse with others, or making negative remarks about your spouse (or ex-spouse) to others, they will learn that this is the way to navigate their relationships. Instead, it is important that your kids witness you clearly, calmly resolving conflicts within your marriage. It is also important that your kids witness a conversation where someone says, "I'm becoming heightened emotionally and need a pause in the conversation to regulate myself." Apologizing to your partner in a heartfelt way in front of your kids is also beautiful.

Your kids need to witness a marriage or relationship that has boundaries, unconditional love, emotional maturity, mutual respect, and security, *consistently*. They need to see you navigate your emotions in a positive way while you also create joy, fun, and laughter together. A marriage is a sacred bond and should be treated as a top priority in your life so your kids can grow up with a functional, nourishing example of what they should seek in their own relationships.

It's not what you say to your kids about relationships that matters; it's about everything they *witness*.

If you want your kids to have healthy, intimate partnerships and if you want to end harmful generational patterns and behaviors, you must place boundaries in your relationship with your parents/siblings/friends/kids to honor and cultivate a healthy, loving, thriving life, *regardless* of what you've been told or conditioned to believe. Honor thy mother and father, yes, but not to the point of the betrayal of the self, your marriage, and your kids' future relationships.

Driven by Ego

I want you to consider why you had your kids in the first place. Was it because you wanted someone to love you unconditionally? Because you wanted a family? Because it felt like the next natural step in your partnership? Because you wanted to create a family that was better than yours? Whatever the answer is, the answer will probably be about you. Not your kids; you. It was about your wants, needs, and desires. Keeping this in mind, you need to consider the prospect that your ego was involved in your decision to have kids, on some level. You probably unconsciously dreamed up some scenario of what life would or should look like once your kids had grown up, based on your own traumas, fears, anxieties, parenting paradigms, and wants and needs.

Your kids are not here to fill your wants and needs. Your attachment to your kids therefore needs to be examined through the lens of whether you've become dependent on your children for fulfilling your unmet needs.

As your children grow into adults (whether they are millennials or Gen Zers), they will have (or will have had) access to the Internet and the ability to google anything. Social media has had both positive and negative impacts on our kids, and one of the bittersweet outcomes of widespread social media use is, many kids are growing to understand the impact their childhoods have had on them. Because of this, today's adults cut their parents off a lot quicker than Gen Xers ever have and are keener to notice toxic and immature adult behaviors, especially after they've had their own children. You may view this as a betrayal, but remember, your adult children are not yours to keep like a trophy on a shelf, or as a reflection of your greatness. They are autonomous beings who are separate from you.

So many parents damage their relationships with their children further by living in the ego and attempting to overpower, punish, control, and micromanage them, or to turn them into mini versions of themselves. Consider whether you might be seeking love and validation from your children through how "worthy" you deem them to be. Conscious parents value their kids for who they are as a human being, not for what they do or accomplish.

Being a conscious parent means going through an ego death. It means not clipping your kids' wings after you've taught them how to fly. We all want our kids to be financially and generally independent, not codependent on us (their parents), so this means their wants, desires, and successes need to belong to them, not their parents (even if you guided them and supported them morally or financially while they tried to obtain their goals, dreams, and aspirations).

To Conclude

Becoming a conscious parent means becoming conscious of yourself. It means finding the wounds you have and healing them. It means checking that ego and how you speak to your kids.

I get it. It's hard work. But I'm here to help. Refer to the types of enmeshment we talked about in Chapter 3 and identify whether you are enmeshed with your kids in any way.

Remember that your kids don't care about your trauma, even if you share it with them — nor should they have to. They may have understanding and compassion for you, but what they ultimately need is a parent who shows up for them in the present moment every day of their lives, regardless of what trauma that parent has experienced. Your trauma should not become theirs, or a reason for why you can't be a better parent to them. Kids need conscious parents that have healed and grown.

If you're a parent of a young adult, remember that forcing your unsolicited opinions onto them may create a divide between you. How they choose to live their life is their decision to make, not yours. Give support and open your heart and home to whoever your children have in their lives. Support their friendships, relationships, wishes, and dreams.

At the end of my life, I want my daughters to know I worked my ass off to become a better parent for them. I want them to be able to see that I made self-improvements, emotionally matured, and did the work all throughout their lives.

You will be ten times more successful in life when you do the work. This is your valor.

7

Coparenting Through Divorce

IN *YOU OUGHTA KNOW* BY Alanis Morissette (also a Gen Xer), Alanis spews the hate and venom she (ostensibly) feels toward her ex. Who didn't relate to that song when it came out, or at least love it? However, contrary to what Alanis says, if you've had a marriage that has failed and led to divorce or separation, then the reason for the relationship breakdown remains yours to heal.

As we have established, many people stay in unhealthy relationships because it feels like home. For example, if you had a childhood filled with cycles of heightened conflict/chaos or emotional immaturity, you are likely to pick a partner who also experienced these circumstances on some level in their own childhood. Because of this, if you are now divorced, it is likely that you and your now-ex initially felt aligned or were trauma-bound because you both experienced emotional/physical trauma, abuse, neglect, abandonment, or parental immaturity in your own childhoods.

Is this the case for you? Think about it.

Oftentimes, parents believe that their ex is the sole reason for their divorce and that they (unlike their ex) emerged unscathed from their childhood. This is (obviously) flat-out denial.

Do you believe this about your divorce? I once did, too.

If you're a child of divorce, think about your divorced parents' patterns and what you're currently repeating with your own children and your ex. Are you trash-talking your ex on the regular in front of your kids? If so, we clearly need to work together so you can create a new coparenting relationship with your ex outside of what is normalized today.

Emotional immaturity and your ego are at play when you befriend your child, compete with your ex, share details about your ex and marriage with your child, or normalize hating your ex or treating your ex poorly in front of your child. These are *all* examples of parenting from an extremely unhealthy place. More to the point, this hurts the child more than anyone else. All you are doing here is weaponizing your ex's missteps. Furthermore, badmouthing your ex, treating your ex with disdain in front of your child, flat-out refusing to communicate with your ex at all, or using your kids as messengers to compensate for the lack of emotional maturity needed to effectively communicate and coparent with your ex are all behaviors that are extremely damaging to children.

Divorced or not, it is important for each parent to foster a loving relationship with the other parent. This is what you should be practicing *and* preaching in front of your kids. This helps your children to understand what appropriate behavior is and isn't, and it gives them a voice when one parent is badmouthing the other (kids are allowed to have boundaries of their own and to love both of their parents).

I'm not recommending "faking it" and wearing a façade whenever you interact with your ex-partner in front of your kids. I *am* recommending having exclusively mature, adult conversations with your ex, whether your kids witness those conversations or not. It's about what's in the best interests of the child, not you.

Do you know how many parent-teacher meetings I've sat in as a teacher where both parents have demeaned the other, constantly competing and positioning themselves as the "better parent?" *Hundreds*. Often, there was eye-rolling and crossed arms, their backs turned slightly away from one another. There were also many meetings where only one parent would be present because the other could no longer stomach being in the same room as them. Other times, both parents would succeed in turning up but would sit at opposite ends of the room, auditorium, or sports field. This happened *countless* times.

How many divorced couples do you know who do this? And it's just normalized! It's "what divorced couples do." Well, listen here: I've been there and done that, and the children are the collateral damage. When a child's parents are emotionally immature, living in survival mode, playing the victim, being ego-based, acting with insecurity, or constantly pulling at the child in an emotional tug-of-war, the child suffers a great deal. Many children in this situation develop anxiety, anger, and depression, to list a few common side-effects. By engaging in this behavior with your ex-partner, the message you're conveying to your child is that half of the child is flawed due to the shortcomings or mistakes of your ex.

It's not your child's responsibility to carry this burden. I repeat: *it's not your child's responsibility to carry this burden*. These matters should remain between the adults so you can allow your child to have a healthy relationship with *both* of you. Your child, no matter what their age, is not your confidant or "best friend," and it's not your job to paint them a picture of who their other parent was during your relationship with them. A child's perception is (and should be) very different to your perception or experience of that person, because the perception of a parent is always very different to the perception of an ex-spouse. This difference needs to be honored so the parent-child relationship can grow. Instead of pointing the finger at your ex, it's your responsibility, as the adult, to heal; to first look at your mistakes, behaviors, and patterns. Without each person involved in the divorce or separation seeking to heal their *own* trauma and unhealthy behavioral patterns, the cycle continues.

The most impactful and beautiful thing you can do for your children (and your ex) is to support your (and their) healing journey. If your child has two mentally healthy, emotionally mature parents, they will greatly benefit in the long run.

If your ex cheated or has narcissistic traits, that's about *them*, and was likely caused by them having a pattern of self-sabotage. Perhaps they felt unworthy of love and were unconsciously creating a situation that felt akin to the parental rejection that felt familiar to them. Alternatively, maybe they use and abuse people before discarding them because they struggle with vulnerability. Regardless, do not burden your children with your partner's mistakes and wounds!

While divorce can destroy a family, it can also be a blessing in disguise: it presents an opportunity for you to understand yourself and why you were attracted to this person from the beginning. Why did they feel like home to you? What were the parts of them that felt familiar; that reminded you of your life as a child? Remember, hurt people hurt people, and healed people heal people.

You can't control others, but you can control you and the way you show up for your kids.

Parent Alienation

Here, I want to discuss a topic that continues to plague many divorced parents today. This is parent alienation.

According to research, Generation X has more divorced parents than any other generation up to this point, so much so that this period is called "the divorce boom."

What does that mean for Gen Xers?

It means many of us witnessed our divorced parents' treatment of each other, including any instances of them speaking poorly of each other, and much more besides. As a result, many of us were probably unconsciously alienated from our parents, and the proof is in the pudding: look at the generational patterns we've created! Look at how Generation X's divorced couples treat one another and the effect this is having on our kids' mental health! This isn't an accident or a coincidence. These are subconscious patterns that have been ingrained from one generation to the next. Our kids weren't born with anxiety and depression; it was created somewhere along the line. Yes, there are genetics involved, but that doesn't make the new generations' record numbers of anxiety and depression okay or normal. So, how do we change this? Well, it starts with everyone who has gone through divorce (or a separation from a partner they had a child with) being intentional about how they treat their coparent.

What does parent alienation look like?

Let's say a child is with their mom for the weekend. After the visit, the dad asks, "How was your weekend?" The child tells them how much fun they had, and the dad says, "That's nice. So, there weren't any problems?" or something along this line of questioning. Now, perhaps there was, in fact, a problem or a conflict the child had with the mom during the visit. Perhaps the mom had to set a boundary or enforce a rule or consequence. The child has, by this point, long moved on from it, but now, it becomes the main focus of the conversation between the dad and child as the child conveys what happened. The dad then tells the child how he wouldn't have done or said what the mother did or said. He then shares what *he* would've done, as the "right way" to handle the situation.

Through this conversation, the child learns to not focus on the fun they had with their mom, but to instead keep score of what went *wrong* during their time with their mom, so they can report to the dad after the visit (as a means of connection).

Perhaps, alternatively, the child talks about all the fun they had with their mom and the dad tells the child that what they did was boring or stupid, or that they'll take them somewhere better. Perhaps the dad becomes visibly upset or disgusted as the child speaks. Perhaps they laugh sarcastically. In this situation, the child learns to manage the emotions of their parent and accordingly filters what they say, so they can receive love and approval.

This leads to the slow, steady decline of the child's relationship with the villainized parent. It also conditions children to play roles and feel responsible for their parents' emotions. They do what they can to avoid triggering the feelings of shame, guilt, or rejection that (unfairly) arise from them loving the other parent.

This is how parent alienation begins to take hold.

Severing (or consistently trying to sever) the relationship between your child and their other parent (perhaps by consistently speaking poorly of them to your child, or telling them they get to choose between parents when they're old enough) is parent alienation and emotional immaturity. As unconscious as it may be, it is extremely damaging to children. Inviting your kids into conversations in which you make fun of or belittle the other parent to feed your ego and insecurities, or to convince your child and yourself that these are valid reasons for the divorce, is extremely damaging to the child. The only one that loses in this situation is the child.

We all have our faults and make mistakes. No one is perfect. Therefore, when parenting mistakes are made, there needs to be grace in allowing a coparent to rectify them and change their behavior. Mistakes should not be viewed as opportunities to kick another human being when they are down. I've witnessed this with many of my clients, and the resultant destruction and trauma is devasting to a child. My plea here is to end parent alienation (which is not a "mistake," but a pattern of behavior) and make things right with your children, even if they're adults. Every child has the right to love both their parents exactly as they are, regardless of how one parent feels about the other parent. We need more love and compassion in this world, and kids need their parents, during childhood and beyond. When they become adults, they will be able to decide what kind of relationship they want with each of their parents, but that should never be decided for them through alienation (which is no better than brainwashing them into hating or disrespecting their parent).

Parent alienation is abuse and should never be dismissed. Unfortunately, there are still countless cases of parent alienation where courts have gotten involved and wrongly aided the parent alienation, especially when a narcissistic parent has been involved. This situation is tragic. The destruction that narcissists leave in their wake in these cases is far-reaching and undeniable. Fortunately, however, more attorneys and judges are becoming aware of these heinous behaviors that are inflicted onto not only parents, but children.

Manifestations of Parent Alienation

Let's summarize everything we have discussed by taking a deeper look at specific examples of what parent alienation can look like.

- "The silver bullet." This is when you call the police or Child Protective Services and make false allegations against the targeted parent. My mother did this to me once, and a client of mine has experienced this as well.
- Not allowing a child to speak to or have daily access to their parent, whether in person or digitally (e.g., over FaceTime).
- Moving to another state or country without the consent or

knowledge of the other parent.

- Manipulating a child's love for and loyalty toward the alienating parent with money and rewards, such as toys or gifts, that are well beyond the normal wants and needs of a child. This is done to make the child view the targeted parent as not loving or "less than."

- Withholding gifts or cards sent to the child's home from the targeted parent.

- Offering more attractive events to a child, such as vacations, in competition with the targeted parent (and then never actually following through on taking the vacation).

- Allowing the use of underage drinking or drug-use and normalizing these behaviors, to make your home more attractive to a teenager/college student and to make the target parent look "too strict" or "rigid."

- Encouraging destructive behaviors toward the alienated parent (e.g., being rude; refusing to visit the target parent; going against the custody agreement; refusing to communicate with the target parent).

- Giving money and rewards to the child when they call a boyfriend/girlfriend/stepparent "Mom" or "Dad."

- Having the child "parrot" you or use the exact same or very similar wording as you regarding the character of the target parent (and cloaking these words as if they came directly from the child).

- Telling outright lies or making exaggerations and false accusations to incentivize the child to act with hostility and to make demeaning remarks toward the alienated parent.

- Posting on social media in a way that disparages the alienated parent (especially when you know the child can see the post).

- Getting the child to idealize you as superior and righteous, with no human flaws, and developing an unhealthy codependency (which only further damages the child's autonomy and their ability to have independent thoughts).

- Speaking on behalf of the child about what the child "wants," rather than what they need (i.e., both parents being in their lives and making decisions that are in the best interests of the child).

- Isolating the alienated parent by reaching out to their family members and friends and telling lies or making exaggerations and false accusations.

- Psychologically manipulating the child so they believe the alienated parent is unsafe or dangerous. This leads to the child displaying anxiety and fear around the alienated parent.

- Lying to the child by saying things like, "If Mom/Dad loved you, they wouldn't have anyone else in their life," (e.g., a significant other), or otherwise suggesting that the alienated parent is not "loyal" to the child.

- Making the child completely codependent on you for every want and need while belittling and demeaning the role and caregiving ability of the alienated parent.

- Parentification (see Chapter 3).

- Withdrawing love and affection from the child when they speak well of the alienated parent. This could include the silent treatment, going into a fit of rage, or stating that you are better than the alienated parent due to "all you've done" for the child.

- Consistently ignoring court orders regarding custody agreements, such as consistently dropping the child off late or consistently asking for more time with the child (to an extent that violates the custody agreement).

- Telling the child that the home of the target parent is not the child's "real home."

- Consistently making plans with the child on days the child is supposed to be with the target parent (according to the court order or custody agreement) without discussing these plans with the target parent first. This makes the child think the target parent is being mean and unreasonable when they do not agree to the plans.

Note that many of the characteristics listed here are narcissistic and, in extreme cases, sociopathic, especially if the offender has a pattern of alienating their children from other partners. Sociopaths have a long historical pattern of manipulating and exploiting their children, making their children codependent on them, and dismissing and violating the rights of the other parent(s) that they've had children with.

Often, children/young adults who have an emotionally immature parent remain in the "freeze" state when they are with that parent. This is why the alienating parent will often find that they don't have any problems at all with the child when they are with them. Then, when the child returns to or spends time with the more "mature" parent (or the "alienated" parent), they transition to the "fight-or-flight" state, because they no longer have to perform and be the "perfect" child in order to remain safe. This means the child may be combative, angry, easily frustrated, anxious, or completely exhausted when they are with the "alienated" parent. They also may want to self-isolate because their nervous system needs time to return to homeostasis. Do not take this personally and also do not ignore it.

Navigating Parent Alienation

Millions of children are alienated from their parents through these methods. Notice the signs and act. Do not allow these things to become commonplace in your family dynamic. If this brainwashing continues into your child's teenage years, they will begin adopting these views as their own.

If this is the situation you're in, contact an attorney who is well-versed in parent alienation. If you need help finding one, reach out to me.

If you know your ex is speaking poorly of you, ignoring what has been written in a custody agreement, or undermining you as a valued parent, do not sit back and ignore it. This will continue to worsen if it is not addressed head-on. Be sure to document every interaction. Even if it's "just" shitty remarks or looks from your ex during the exchange time that take place in front of your kids, call it out, but not in front of your children, if you can avoid it. Instead, discuss the behaviors with the other parent the next time you have an opportunity to do so. If it continues in front of the children, make the alienating parent aware that you will be establishing new boundaries in front of your children regarding what behavior is and isn't acceptable during exchanges or extracurricular events.

One of my many regrets is not involving attorneys to address my ex's violation of our divorce agreement when I had the chance. Don't make the same mistake that I did!

If an ex is using your kids as a messenger to deliver any kind of information that you know should be communicated directly to you, do not allow it. This puts the child in a role that doesn't belong to them. Adult decisions and communication belong between adults, period. Communicating through your child instead of having direct coparenting conversations is immature and manipulative behavior. Kids forget information, convey the message in their own words, and are also left to deal with the emotional reaction of the receiving parent. This is far from appropriate. If you are ever the recipient of such a message, let your child deliver it and then draw a boundary, letting them know that such information needs to be delivered by the other parent in future, that you will reiterate this to them, and that they should not deliver messages on behalf of the other parent moving forward. Tell them that if they are asked to do it again, they should let the parent in question know that they should talk to you instead. Repeat this again and again, if need be, and then address it head-on with the other parent. Make sure to document this as well, in case you need to provide this information to professionals (e.g., attorneys, a court, or law guardians).

Remind your children of the custody agreement ordered by the judge. Most agreements have general language with regards to making disparaging remarks about the other parent in front of the children. If the behavior does not change, let your children know that the other parent is violating the custody agreement when they do this. It's important that your children know what mature, healthy behaviors are and aren't.

If lies are being told about you by the other parent and your child repeats one to you, let your child know simply that it's not true—no further explanation needed. If your child begins to doubt whether you are capable as a parent, make sure you do not behave in a way that makes this doubt seem valid, and reaffirm love and trust.

If you notice you are being alienated, calmly tell the other parent that you'd prefer it if they didn't roll their eyes and treat you so poorly in front of the kids (or whatever the "alienating" behavior seems to be), and walk away. Do not give the alienating parent a chance to respond or engage any further. Just drop the little seed in front of your kids. This achieves many goals. It shows your children you can be calm even during a conflict. It builds safety and security with you. It also shows your children that it's okay to stand up for yourself, and it shows your children what emotionally immature behavior is and what it isn't. Above all, it plants a seed inside them that tells them they have the power to love both their parents, despite their parents' differences.

There are now apps designed for coparents' communication, and I highly recommend only communicating with your coparent on such a platform if you suspect they are attempting to alienate you from your children. Everything you say and communicate should be in writing in some shape or form — otherwise, it can be easily denied — and such apps document every conversation in one location. For a small fee, the entire conversation can also be downloaded and converted into a PDF if needed.

Here is a list of actions you should take if you suspect you are being alienated by another parent:

- Document, document, document!
- Don't have conversations with the alienator over the phone. Communicating in writing allows you time to pause, think, and respond when you are emotionally regulated. It also allows you to document everything that's said.
- Use AppClose to text and communicate with your coparent. This app keeps texts in one location for free.
- Keep conversations short, to the point, and focused on the children and their education, medical needs, and extracurriculars.
- Read the custody agreement ordered by the court to your children and reassure them that they have the right to love both of their parents.
- Set boundaries with your children by letting them know that adult matters are to be discussed among adults, and that this will remain to be the case until the children turn eighteen (and no sooner).
- Give your children the language they need to inform each parent of their boundaries. Tell them that if either parent has a problem

or concern, the child can say, "This belongs between you and Mom/Dad."

- Surround yourself with other adults who speak highly of you and love you in front of your children, to show your children that not everyone shares the feelings and thoughts that the alienator does.

- Get support from parent alienation groups on social media and set up a self-care routine, so you can be the best you can to yourself and your children.

- Stay in contact with your attorney and share your documentation regularly, even if you think disparaging remarks or demeaning facial expressions aren't a big deal. Do not dismiss these behaviors, especially if they occur in front of your children. You are building a case of a pattern of behavior.

- The preteen and teenage years are when the alienation and brainwashing begin to really take hold, and this is also when children feel they have the right to "choose" which parent to live with. However, remember that children are not legally adults until they are eighteen and that the brain doesn't fully develop until the age of twenty-five. You are allowed to "block" decisions by your teenaged children that could alter or damage the course of their life, especially if the decision has been made due to a temporary disagreement.

Never accept less than you deserve from a coparent. Do not accept poor, immature behavior in front of your children and dismiss it by reasoning that "that's just who the other parent is." I would also suggest that if you find yourself being the target of parent alienation, you research and contact a counselor for your children. Children need a place to vent about both of their parents so they can process their circumstances and learn what healthy and appropriate behavior from adults looks like.

In my situation, my ex was completely against my daughters going to counseling, which was a problem (because I needed his consent). Need I say that it's a red flag if your ex discourages their children from seeking counseling after a divorce? My daughters had been exposed to divorce, my mother's narcissist abuse, and the fallout of how that abuse had affected me, and they needed support. What should you do in this situation? You should keep showing up for your kids. Keep being the kind, beautiful you that you are in front of your children and ex. Keep putting boundaries in place and stick to them consistently. The boundaries are for you, not for them.

Do not allow others to control your emotions and the way in which you respond. Notice I didn't say "react" here. There's a difference between reacting and responding. You must emotionally detach yourself from your ex enough to be able to observe their behavior and give a controlled response, not a reaction. Need help with this? I've got you! Let the coparent know that you will be calling their behavior out in front of the kids; that these are the boundaries you are setting moving forward; that you will act according to the custody agreement and these boundaries. If they ask if you are threatening them, let them know the only threat being made is one to their ego.

If you cannot count on the alienating parent to show up maturely, then contact your attorney with all your documentation and have them write a letter asking for the alienating parent to cease and desist with the behaviors in front of the children. If the alienating parent then continues with these behaviors, they are violating the court order for custody. If that doesn't help, then decide on a mutual location where you do not have to interact in front of your children for exchanges.

One thing is for sure: you should not wait years and years for someone to change their behavior toward you, especially when this mistreatment occurs in front of your children. This only enables the behavior, and unfortunately, it's possible (in fact, very likely) that your children will eventually model these behaviors as well. Set boundaries and be the example of emotional maturity that your kids need.

Alienating parents need to be held accountable for their emotional immaturity and the lasting impact their actions have on their children (and the generations to come). Where will you be holding yourself accountable on these matters? What changes will you make for your children? How will you move things forward with your coparent and child?

Taking Responsibility for Effective Coparenting

For me, it is my number one priority to truly listen to my daughters and understand what they genuinely need. As a parent, this is what emotional maturity, compassion, empathy, self-regulation, and showing up as the leader in their life looks like, and you should practice these traits regardless of what your ex thinks or says about you. My wish for you is that you will take something from my lessons in life and be courageous enough to admit that you're responsible for your side of the street; for the hurt you've created for your child and ex. After all, regardless of your current feelings toward your ex, something beautiful was created between the two of you: your children. Recognize the good qualities your ex has, no matter how hard that may be, and focus on them. Your love for your child needs to outweigh your hatred of your ex.

You are probably a parent who wants a better life for their kids, but if your kids don't have parents who can admit to their mistakes, make heartfelt apologies, recognize their own patterns of behavior, or show up for the kids with a consistently regulated nervous system and unconditional love, how can you possibly give them a better life than yours? Children are only children for a short amount of time in the grand scheme of their life, and eventually, they'll awaken to the impact you've had on them (positive or negative). What's more, that impact can (and probably will) continue for a lifetime, if left unhealed, and if they become parents, the unhealed patterns will likely continue through the generations. So, be the leader in your child's life that they need. If you want them to be responsible for their actions, take ultimate responsibility for your actions with your ex and get on the same page with them, so you can effectively coparent.

Some of you might be asking, "What if I'm on a healing journey and my ex isn't?" I want you to know that I've been there, too. If you're in that position right now, remember that while you can share information with your ex about how they can start their healing journey, they simply may not be open to healing, talking to a professional, or taking a serious look at themselves, their lack of emotional immaturity, or their childhood yet. They may feel they know everything they need to know about themselves and "that's the end of the story." You can't convince someone else to make changes, even if them not changing impacts your children. All you can do is hold true to yourself and believe in yourself and your power to not only heal yourself, but to also show your children that healing is possible and that people can change.

I have been on my own healing journey for a while now, and my daughters have seen drastic changes in how I parent, communicate with them, honor them, respect them, and validate their perspectives and current reality. I share with them the tools that have helped me and I model emotional maturity in front of them, regardless of how I'm treated by their other parent. That's true emotional maturity and valor.

Albert Einstein once said that insanity can be defined as doing the same thing repeatedly and expecting a different result, and this applies to every area of our lives, including our relationship with our kids and our exes.

Let your children know that it's okay and appropriate for them to love

Denise Conde

both of their parents, and give your children permission to voice how their parents' behaviors affect them. Teach your children to say, "This is between you and Mom/Dad," whenever they hear one parent badmouthing the other. It's not a child's job to manage the emotions of adults, and putting the responsibility to communicate and coparent effectively back on the adult takes the child out of the equation.

Perhaps you're asking, "When is an appropriate time to have this conversation with a child?" The answer is, immediately! If they can speak, then give them the language they need to express their feelings.

We need to model mature behaviors as parents, take accountability for any mistakes we make and shortcomings we have, and change our behavior toward our children moving forward. That's maturity and accountability, and that's the very foundation of any healthy coparenting relationship.

Remember that you can't control others, but you can control you. Most of all, believe in yourself and know in your heart that you are powerful, that you can do hard things, and that your children love you.

Stay on your path and your journey. Like I mentioned before, we all make mistakes and hurt others (intentionally or unintentionally), but if we don't acknowledge these behaviors within ourselves and others, we only perpetuate the divorce cycle into the next generation.

Let's look at what some mature and effective means of coparenting are:

- Having the same routine, rules, and structure in both homes for bedtime, breakfast, lunch, dinner, homework, extracurriculars, phone time, and so on. Consistency is key.
- Not making negative or disparaging remarks about your ex to your children, even if your child is complaining about the other parent. In this situation, let your child know that you've heard them and understand how hard the situation must be for them. You can help guide your child through conflict by framing it as an

opportunity to place boundaries and grow the relationship further.

- Stating your boundaries with the coparent. For example, if the coparent raises their voice on the phone, hang up and only communicate through text. This also allows you to document what is being said and gives both of you the opportunity to slow the conversation down and dedicate time to formulating productive responses, so you can reach an agreement on the matter at hand.

- (Assuming the house isn't literally on fire) taking your time with responses. Give yourself time to pause, rather than giving in to a kneejerk reaction. When you feel dysregulated, state, "I will get back to you on this." Period. Give yourself time to think about what is in the best interests of the child instead of trying to spite the other parent.

- Understanding that the coparent sees you the way they want to see you. Do not try to convince the other parent that they should see you the way you think you deserve to be seen. This is where actions speak louder than words and into your character and integrity. You decide how you act and respond. Do not give that power to anyone else.

- Acknowledging the patterns in the coparenting relationship. Are there long texts exchanged and arguing throughout the day, with insults thrown back and forth? Did this exist in the marriage before the breakup? Are you perpetuating the cycle by participating in it?

- Understanding that adults are allowed to have disagreements and can handle disappointment. This is where boundaries come into play. If you're in an over-the-phone argument, end the call and choose to not participate. Text and state that since the conversation has become heated, you're going to be leaving it until both parties are calm. Take the time you need to cool off. Like, really cool off. For many of us, that takes at least an hour, if not more. Allow yourself the time to formulate a response that is child-centered and not a personal attack.

- Sticking to the divorce agreement. Allow for slight flexibility but take note of any worrying patterns. If the coparent insists on you making unreasonable allowances, remind them that while you might have agreed to these in the past, you will be adhering to the divorce (custody) agreement moving forward. If the coparent sends a barrage of reasons for why the child needs more time with them, take that as an indication that if you don't put an end to this line of thought, the situation could possibly get worse.

- Understanding that even though you may no longer love your coparent, your child does, and that your new significant other (if you have one) is not to make negative remarks about the child's other parent to the child. That's not their place. A significant other does not take the place of the other parent. Even if you wish you'd had your child with this new love, you didn't. Honor that.

- Effectively and maturely communicating all medical, educational, and extracurricular information about the child to the coparent, even if they don't return the favor. Do not match this immaturity. Act with integrity and stick to the custody agreement.

- Making attempts for your children to see the two of you sitting together or talking at their performances, milestone events, or sporting events, even just for a short time. This shows your children that both parents are invested in their lives. Call a truce at events that are centered around the children. They are not about the divorce, custody battle, or negative feelings you hold toward each other.

- Focusing on the good qualities of the coparent. If you feel your coparent is a narcissist and that's all you see in them, that's likely all that you'll ever see. Showing gratitude for even the tiniest of things goes a long, long way. Even if you only write these things in a gratitude journal or say them silently to yourself, gratitude is a beautiful practice.

- Normalizing taking pictures together during your child's milestone events. Remember, these events are about the child and their accomplishments, even if you've helped your child to achieve that accomplishment more than the coparent has (or vice versa). Do not diminish the role of the other parent. It's not a competition. Both parents deserve to be a part of their child's milestones and celebrations.

- Putting the needs of the children first and setting aside any ill will toward your coparent.

- Loving your child more than you hate your ex. Break the negative patterns that existed during your relationship.

The most beautiful things coparents can do for their children include getting along, being open to having conversations as a united, cooperative team, and discussing important topics in person, when necessary, in front of the kids. I know of several coparenting couples who will even get together for the holidays, birthday parties, and special events at one of their homes or a neutral location. This is a whole other level of coparenting that takes a great deal of emotional maturity and for both of you to accept that while the marriage didn't work, there's no reason to be enemies.

I'm proud of moments like these that my daughters have experienced, and I celebrate the many divorced couples who have been able to see beyond their own egos; who have realized that it's truly in the children's best interests for them to work together and display healthy, mature coparenting.

Lastly, if you've been alienated from your child, remember that regardless of what your child has said to you, they do love you. No one can break that bond. If your relationship is wobbly because of it, never give up hope for reunification. If you know where they are, send them a letter or a card, not to bash the other parent or to tell "your side" of the story, but to remind them that you love them. Keep it short and simple. This shows who is the healthier, more mature parent. Invite them on any vacations you may take or to holiday get-togethers, even if they are rejecting you. It's the thought and consideration that matters. Send them meaningful gifts even if you think the alienator might be throwing them away and document it by taking a picture (in case they claim you never reached out). Remind them of the good times you've shared together, to show them that the entire relationship wasn't "bad." Share special events, sayings, jokes, funny times, or special moments that the two of you shared.

Above all, never make a child, even if they are an adult (i.e., over the age of eighteen), responsible for what occurred or choices that they made in order to stay safe. It wasn't their fault.

Most importantly, take care of you! Take care of your body, mind, and soul, so that if and when they do return to you, you are the healthiest version of yourself that they most definitely need.

You've got this. Remember you are loved.

8

Forgiveness and Spirituality

Nature's first green is gold,
Her hardest hue to hold.
Her early leaf's a flower;
But only so an hour.
Then leaf subsides to leaf.
So Eden sank to grief,
So dawn goes down to day.
Nothing gold can stay.

—*Nothing Gold Can Stay*, Robert Frost[7]

THIS POEM HAS BEEN ONE of my favorites ever since I read *The Outsiders* by S. E. Hinton in high school. What I love about it is the observation that nature's first green is gold. To me, this relates to both nature and humans. When we are first born, we are green, new, and

[7] Frost, R. (1923): *Nothing gold can stay. The Yale Review, 12*(2), 108-109. Retrieved from poetryfoundation.org on December 2, 2024
(www.poetryfoundation.org/poems/148652/nothing-gold-can-stay-5c095cc5ab679).

beautiful, like gold. However, gold is nature's (and humans') hardest hue to hold, because, just like a seedling, everything continues to grow and change with the seasons of life.

While along our path we will meet people who have both negative and positive impacts on us, I have to disagree on a certain level with Robert Frost when he says that nothing gold can stay. In the very depths of every one of us, I believe there is gold to be unearthed again: our authentic selves. Yet the Gen Xer who has been traumatized has aged into something or someone that they are not at their very core. They've become something that's based on their conditioning and subconscious. They've become who they've been told they are; who they needed to become while they were living in survival mode.

Now, you have the choice to undo this damage.

The beauty of the universe is that every day and at every present moment, you truly have a choice to start again; to recreate your life and become who you want to be, step by step. The past doesn't define you. It's not a life sentence, unless you choose to make it one. We know that constantly living in the past recreates the past in our future, and that we can make a conscious choice to dig deep and learn about ourselves on a personal level, thereby ending this cycle. Just because someone once made a mistake or lived their life a certain way doesn't mean there's not a new way to live out the remaining days of their life waiting to be discovered.

We know that our thoughts are so powerful that our nervous system doesn't know the difference between the past and what's happening in real time in our minds.

Underline that sentence and think about it.

Clearly, we need to be aware of our thoughts if we want to intentionally craft our lives. We need to allow the thought to be there; to recognize it and feel it, with the intention of only letting it be there for a certain amount of time.

Intentionally allow yourself to sit with your feelings and thoughts. Start thinking about where your thoughts go off to and how long they stay there for. Is it an hour? A whole day? Have you been thinking the same thoughts for weeks and months? What do you spend most of your time thinking about, and then what shows up in your world?

Only you can answer that question.

Forgiveness

For a long time, there was one integral part of my journey that I was missing: I needed to bring forgiveness into my heart. I knew that to move forward, I needed to let go of all the stories about my traumas that I rehashed in therapy sessions and conversations with my husband.

Forgiveness doesn't mean giving those that have done damage in your life a free pass. To me, it means understanding that everyone's walk in life is different, with different lessons to learn from for growth. It's a dedication to releasing yourself from the past.

Everyone's journey to forgiveness is different and very, very personal. There's no deadline on forgiveness, and if you are never able to forgive someone for the way they hurt you, I get it. Truly.

When you begin to forgive yourself for the mistakes you made when you were in survival mode, you inevitably become able to start forgiving others, taking the actions of others less personally, and looking at others through a compassionate lens (rather than a lens of constant judgment, or perhaps even hatred). You begin to view others through the lens of, "What happened to them?" rather than, "Wow, they must be crazy."

Forgiveness doesn't always mean allowing people who did you harm back into your life. That's what boundaries are for. However, learning to let go of pain and hurt does your body, mind, and soul a world of good, and above all, it allows you to move forward. I don't know if I'll ever speak to my mother or sisters again, but I do hold forgiveness and love for them in my heart.

You have a choice regarding who you include in your life and who you don't. Protect your energy and heart first by combining your boundaries with forgiveness.

Spirituality

Often, when I talk to people about what I do in the realm of spirituality, including holding spiritual sacred ceremonies, they reply that it sounds like "hippy shit." This really makes me giggle with excitement to share more. Let's get deep into what the mystics have known for centuries.

I found that when I was in therapy, it kept me rooted in the past. Having to recount traumatic events and keep my counselor up to date was ineffective for my growth. This isn't a dig at counselors, as mine served me well and gave me the validation that I needed at the time; it's just that the idea is to ultimately no longer need a counselor or therapist, isn't it?

The difference between what a therapist does and what I do as a mentor is, I keep my clients moving forward, rather than keeping them rooted in the past. The past needs to be revisited and integrated into the present, but there is also a transition from the past that needs to happen if you are going to be present and embrace a bright future. Life is full of lessons, and if you are mindful of these and your own patterns of behavior, the lesson will be learned, and there will no longer be any need to obsess over or contemplate the past.

Humans are not unique in the fact that they exhibit patterns. Everything on this earth has a rhythm, from the instinctual behavioral patterns of an elephant or a dolphin, to a flower's beautiful petals, to the pattern in the rhythm and melody of songs, to the symmetry of seashells' etchings. There's another quote attributed to Albert Einstein in which he talks about the fact that one of the greatest human tragedies is that humans believe they are separate from the universe. Humans are not separate. We are part of a collective. It's just that too many of us become spiritually disconnected from what the universe and the earth have to offer us.

What are you currently doing to connect to nature and the earth? Think about this and write your answer down. If your answer is, "I'm not doing anything to connect," and you want to learn more about how to do so, I've got you! Go to my website (www.deniseconde.com), where you will find a link to the *Earthing* movie and a link to purchase *Earthing* products, to inspire you to get started right away.

Scientists are now able to prove that everything vibrates, including you and me, and we know that the vibes and energy we give off are felt by others. This is measurable. You can walk into a room and feel the vibe before anyone even says a word. You can control this vibration of yours through meditation, breathwork, yoga, and so on.

Will you be the one in the room bringing the vibe up or down? Or will you be the one to match the vibe, so you can fit in? I say turn that energy up and let others match you! You are divine, so let it shine. Inside my courses, I discuss which specific meditations work best for this.

We know that what is happening on the inside of us is reflected on the outside, and vice versa. For example, we often feel chaotic inside when there is chaos in our homes or workspaces. My laundry and paperwork are where my disorganization screams chaos. Where is your chaos? Write your answer down. Do it right now. Really think about your home. That is the perfect place to start: clearing out the clutter in your mind and heart and in your home.

Alternatively, perhaps you only feel in control and at peace when your home is absolutely perfect, and you are triggered by anything not being exactly where it's supposed to be. Some call this OCD, and this tends to come from a place of childhood neglect, or an unconscious pattern passed onto you that no longer belongs to you.

Where are you on this spectrum? Think about it and acknowledge it. Bring awareness to this and then intentionally choose balance.

When you take intentional steps to create peace of mind, slow down, and get quiet (rather than trying to control everyone and everything), you become more open, you create space to let new ideas and information in, and you grow much more receptive to life. There is ease and flow, just like the natural flow of a river, rather than resistance.

If you are religious, it is important that you keep practicing, or find a new spiritual practice that serves you and resonates with you. This can prove challenging for some: many of us Gen Xers have been manipulated using religion, or have been convinced we will burn in hell if we don't follow a certain set of religious rules (I, for one, am yet to see anyone spontaneously combust for breaking these standards). Victims of this tend to lose all sense of their own spirituality, because it was used to manipulate, shame, and guilt them during their childhood.

If this has happened to you, I totally understand. I rejected any type of religion for a long time for these exact reasons. I have, however, adopted a spiritual practice that fits me since then, and I suggest you do the same.

A few years ago, I decided to go to my childhood local church with my husband, who had started attending again. I'll never forget the moment during the sermon when the pastor said, "Those that heal, serve others on their healing journey." I felt like he was speaking directly to me. These are the synchronicities that occur in life, if we are paying attention.

Even though this was a profound moment in my life, I knew that the monotonous rituals involved in that church and being called a sinner repeatedly just didn't sit right with me. (No judgment to others and their practices by any means.) The word "sin" sounds like another word for shame or guilt to me. Rather than sins, I like to think of our missteps as unconscious mistakes we make along our journey — missteps that are there to force us to grow and learn. We can't grow and heal unless we make mistakes and face failure.

A friend of mine and my husband's was over one night, and he mentioned the word "manifestation." For some reason, the word hung in my mind for days. I finally decided to begin researching the word, and came across a spiritual healer on social media. He offered a free three-day mastermind, which changed everything for me. This led to my first spiritual awakening. It happened during a breathwork sound bowl meditation. I could feel pressure in very specific areas of my body. Shortly after, I realized this was my chakras opening.

Everyone's experiences with breathwork are different, but my life changed drastically after that. I was already on my healing journey, but something shifted inside me from that point, driving me to hire a mentor.

This was no random mentor. She was someone I knew in childhood and my teenage years, and her social media posts resonated with me. I reached out to her, and we worked together for over a year, continuing and deepening both of our healing journeys.

Our lives nearly paralleled one another's when it came to our trauma and chosen careers. This is no weird coincidence. This was serendipity. Fate. Destiny. Divine intervention. We both knew and felt this. I'm forever grateful to her, as well as for the work of Bob Proctor and Sandy Gallagher.

Take steps to overcome your fear of religious damnation by picking a spiritual practice and forming a routine around it that fits where you are now. There are common themes among all spiritual practices, whether you believe in God, the Universe, karma, or something else. Many religions and spiritual practices also focus on forgiveness — forgiving yourself and others. The difference between religion and spirituality is, religion is a set of organized beliefs and practices, while spirituality focuses on individual practices centered around peace and purpose.

If you're looking to become more spiritually aligned, I highly suggest looking on YouTube for spiritual advisors that resonate with you. In addition to Bob Proctor's work, Michael Beckwith is someone I find to be beautifully spiritually aligned. I also offer guidance on spiritual practices that I have created and which have brought me home to my soul's purpose. Check them out on my on my website.

I believe in the existence of something bigger than myself in this universe. I believe in healing and spiritual awakenings, too, because I've experienced both of these things on various levels, as I continue to heal and better myself everyday (it's just the process of all the pieces falling into place). I also know and surround myself with others who have experienced much of the same.

You can choose your own attitudes and beliefs in all areas of your life. You can define and redefine your beliefs and core values and live by them. You must believe that you have this choice, though. If you believe that healing is not possible for you, you will prove yourself right.

What do you believe is obtainable for you? You are a being with a soul who is deserving of love and good things, period. Do you believe that? I hope so, because it's true.

What is that internal nudge inside you that you've perhaps been ignoring? When will you begin to take inspired action on your own behalf? What are your unfulfilled dreams?

We have no idea how much time we have left, so take time away from your day-to-day life, sit outside, listen to your heart, and give that internal nudge a voice. Focus on what you want in your life rather than what you don't want. Open yourself up to the possibility of making that life real for yourself.

Everything is meant to evolve and change. A tree doesn't stop growing and evolving, does it? You can cut away its branches and force it to grow in the direction you want it to, but it doesn't stop growing. It evolves and changes, just like you and me. My mentor also told me many times that a tree doesn't try to pick up its leaves and put them back on after the season has changed and the leaves have fallen away. A tree doesn't look back at what it once was. It continues to grow and evolve.

The changes you make here can be small, but every little one has a ripple effect, and that process starts with you, in your valor. Every little step adds up to the results you are looking for. Even if your dreams don't show up in your reality immediately, that doesn't mean they won't eventually become manifested. You must believe that your efforts and small steps will add up to one big quantum leap.

Do you believe it's too late for you and you're too old because you are a Gen Xer? I call bullshit. Do you find yourself comparing your growth and life to others? Comparison is a killer. Stop doing it. Your journey and path are unique to you. You are exactly where you are meant to be.

Change is inevitable, and if you are focused on reliving the eighties and nineties because they were "a better time in your life," or saying that the younger generations are weak and not tough "like you were," you are not accepting your growth or theirs.

I love the music from our generation (and the hair and trends, too!). Just like the smalltown girl livin' in a lonely world, I won't ever stop believin' in humanity. I hope we can hold onto our youth *and* stop judging and criticizing the growth of other generations.

Many of us had to be tough and rigid in order to survive, and I ask you, how is that toughness affecting your heart, body, and soul? How is it serving you now? Where is your softness, tenderness, and compassion for yourself or others?

Everything can still turn to gold when you turn your heart toward spirituality, tenderness, and forgiveness. "Stay gold, Ponyboy," as Johnny from *The Outsiders* would say.

157

9

Waiting on the World to Change

W E KNOW THAT CHANGE BEGINS with one single person creating a ripple effect, like a drop in the ocean. I am here to tell you that *you* are the drop to create the ripple and to influence future generations.

To catalyze this impact, your healing needs to be undertaken through a multifaceted approach. The neuroscientific evidence that backs this up is out there. Since we've learned trauma is stored in the body, the traditional method of talk therapy and talk therapy *only* has ended. So, why isn't this all over mainstream media? Listen to and read the lyrics from *Waiting on the World to Change* by John Mayer (another shoutout to that Gen Xer! Woot, woot!). That should explain a lot!

Enough said!

Let me ask you this: has your general physician ever told you to try regulating your nervous system? Or to get out in nature? To connect to your spirituality? Has your counselor or therapist?

Bueller? Bueller?

Our mainstream media focuses on getting the population to pop pills and diet. Just look at the commercials for any given ailment or dis-ease. I don't know about you, but those commercials and the "solution's" list of side-effects have me running for the hills! I'm not judging by any means — as discussed in previous chapters, I have been on antidepressants and anti-anxiety medication — but still, many of us drop a pill to alleviate the symptoms without healing the underlying dis-ease. We have become programmed by society to look for something outside of us to heal us, when actually, we have the power to do much of our healing on our own, from within us. The neuroscience is out there and gaining momentum every day. Dr. Bessel van der Kolk said it best:

> ...drugs cannot 'cure' trauma; they can only dampen the expression of a disturbed physiology. And they do not teach the lasting lesson of self-regulation.[8]

Deepak Chopra, Dr. Nicole Lepera, Dr. Bessel van der Kolk, Dr. Joe Dispensa, and so many others discuss at length the connection between inflammation and a dysregulated nervous system. The evidence is everywhere, if you look for it. What results from this is autoimmune disease, such as rheumatoid arthritis and irritable bowel symptoms.

After my father passed away, it was not only the grief itself but the way my family handled it that made the situation as traumatic as it was. Very quickly, my knees became so inflamed that I could barely walk anymore. My cortisol levels (stress hormones) were off the charts, and of course, I was unaware of this. I was young — in my mid-forties. (I had many knee injuries from playing soccer, and the body will attack the most vulnerable parts of the body when traumatized repeatedly.) I went the traditional way (to the orthopedic doctor) and had X-rays, MRIs, injection after

---

[8] van der Kolk, B. (2014): *The Body Keeps the Score*. Viking Books (p. 226).

injection, and, finally, surgery, but none of it actually gave me the relief I wanted or was looking for.

I'm not saying that traditional medicine doesn't serve a purpose. The magic lies in knowing what purpose you wish it to serve.

Did any of my doctors ask me if I'd experienced something traumatic? No, of course not. This is a problem, because like I said, healing requires a multifaceted approach.

My physical therapist at the time consistently said that "motion is lotion," and that stuck with me and kept me moving, even though I was inflamed and in pain. Breathwork, massages, meditation, yoga, and reiki practitioners, along with holistic nutritionists and holistic chiropractors, do *not* get enough credit, and that's largely because many of these practices are based on the knowledge that the body keeps the score in one sense or another.

If these practices are so effective, why don't most insurance companies cover them? Well, you weren't born yesterday, so I'm sure you know why!

As I write, I'm fifty-two years old, and through my own healing of trauma via the aforementioned methods, the inflammation in my knees has greatly decreased, to the point where I am now able to ski with my daughters and husband. Am I a miracle case? No. I did the work and I asked for help (and got it). My friend, who is a certified integrative nutrition health coach and a holistic cancer coach, healed herself of breast cancer. Get a Gen X friend like *that*!

If you're considering getting a counselor or a therapist, be sure to do your homework on who you select. Many are trained and schooled like a general practitioner in a catchall system, but the most effective counselor, therapist, coach, or mentor will be the one who has done the work of healing themselves. *Those* are your people. Look at *Good Will Hunting*. Why was the therapy so effective for Will (Matt Damon)? Because he and Sean (Robin Williams)—the therapist—had similar backgrounds. They were able to relate to one another at a human level, and they even challenged one another to grow. Yes, this is a movie, but it's a perfect example of why clients often don't connect with their therapist or mentor, like the many Will worked with before going to Sean.

This is all part of the hero's journey. Something huge that completely upends us and bring us to our knees, whether a divorce, death, job loss, unhealthy partner, or blowup with family members, usually happens at least once in our lives. This can even just be you reaching the end of your rope and getting tired of your own shit. Whatever it is, there is a great lesson to be learned in that event, and if it's not learned, the universe will present the lesson again and again through another person or circumstance. The universe will tell you to keep looking and searching within yourself for the answers, because the answers *are* within you. You know yourself and your story better than anyone else. That's why self-healing is so powerful.

The universe will also bring great people into your life to help you along the way. All you must do is ask for "your people" and they will show up in some way, shape, or form, whether through a book, movie, or social media post, or (what you consider to be) a random face-to-face interaction. I could recite the exact order of every single book I read when I started my healing journey, and make no mistake, I was manifesting them one right after another. When you ask, the universe shifts to deliver.

Being out in nature and taking in the true beauty and awe of this universe will oftentimes bring you the answers you are searching for, too. When you're able to quiet your mind and observe all that's around you, you come to realize that this universe is abundant with everything you need and is guiding you. There is only one of you — only one person with your unique story and with the power of a fiery phoenix rising out of the ashes.

Opening up, being vulnerable, and asking for help seems unreasonable and difficult for so many of us who hail from Gen X. We learned to figure shit out on our own—and we've survived up until this point, haven't we? But aren't you done with surviving?

One particular quote by Dr. Scott Barry Kaufman is very fitting here. He said, "I have found that one of the most powerful coaching questions is simply, 'Aren't you capable of more?'" [9]

Well, aren't you?

When you're willing to ask for help, I will be here for you. We all deserve to have lives full of peace, love, harmony, ease, joy, and bliss. When you allow for healing, you allow for creativity within your mind.

You are so brilliant and have so many gifts to share with the world.

I had a dysfunctional family during childhood and into adulthood, but I continued to ask for inner peace within myself and the lives of my daughters and husband. Is everything picture-perfect all the time? No, of course not. It's not supposed to be. But I am quantum leaps away from where I was. Old patterns will occasionally emerge, but now, I'm able to understand the lesson, and my mindset isn't, *Why is this happening to me?* but, *This lesson is happening* for *me*.

When you begin your healing journey (which you already have by purchasing this book!), don't be surprised when doors begin to open for you and bring you more and more clarity. There will be little whispers from the universe when this happens, so listen carefully to how you're being guided.

There is great valor in being a Gen Xer. I'm here to take your hand and to walk through it with you. I've invested in myself repeatedly and will continue to do so. When are you going to take that quantum leap for yourself?

I had a counselor for two years while I was also working with a

[9] Posted on December 8, 2022, by @scottbarrykaufman. [Instagram Post]. Please see www.instagram.com/p/Cl6oVGyOkCl

psychologist family member for a few months. I also bought an online course. *After* all of that, I hired my mentor. Why did I do all that? Because I wanted to heal, get unstuck, and create new, healthy patterns so I could live the life I knew I truly deserved to. I had no idea that when I began my healing journey, I'd one day be writing my story, creating courses, and opening my own business to guide others Gen Xers on their healing journey and empower them to heal themselves.

Speaking of my courses, here's a deeper look at my courses and what they can do for you — yes, *you*! Every one of us is in a different stage of our journey, so to make things easy and more attainable, you can purchase the courses that are related to the areas you'd most like to work on.

I am certified to hold spiritual sacred ceremonies, and I am also a sound healer (I use crystal sound bowls). Healing is very effective in a community setting, so keep an eye out for these on my Facebook account (Denise Conde), Instagram (@your.valor), and website (www. deniseconde.com).

Let's recap all the key steps to leaning into your valor as a Gen Xer in this book. These steps align with the different courses I offer, so you can pick and choose what area you'd like to improve upon next.

Gratitude

We've all been told that we should just be grateful for all that we have. Some of us have been conditioned to believe that we don't deserve more or better. But we do! Being grateful means living and breathing the attitude of gratitude, and my course explains why this is so important. This course is free and can be found on my website www.deniseconde.com.

Resurrect the Nervous System

Many neuroscientists will tell you that inflammation is the main cause of nearly every disease, and regulating the nervous system is paramount to decreasing inflammation in your body. So, I've been on the search for the easiest and fastest way to reduce inflammation, and I believe in the *Earthing* movement so much that I've become an affiliate.

As you know, when you are dysregulated, your nervous system becomes stuck in one of the four states: "fight," "flight," "fawn," or "freeze." You develop coping mechanisms (such as overdrinking, drug-use, overeating, and more) to help self-soothe, and over a long period of time, this wreaks havoc on your body. If you've experienced trauma in your childhood or adulthood, have a stressful job, or are in a dysfunctional relationship, it is imperative that you resurrect the nervous system for the longevity of your lifespan. In my course, I discuss at length the four nervous system states, how to move the body out of these states, and the importance of the vagus nerve. This course is also free and can be found on my website www.deniseconde.com and on Instagram (@your.valor).

Respect the Pause

This course is focused on how to identify your emotional triggers (i.e., a response that does not match the event itself in intensity) and suppressed anger, so you can stop reacting with words that you later regret and instead respond with kindness and compassion. This course is prerecorded and short but so, so effective at getting individuals to recognize their own triggers and overcome them. Jump over to my website to grab this, should it sound like a fit for you.

The Subconscious

Here, we discuss how the subconscious mind is developed from birth, how you've allowed the unconscious to rule your life (from your intimate relationships to your beliefs about yourself), and how to rebuild the subconscious. You will learn the impact of trauma reenactment, how to navigate conflicts, the art of listening, how to communicate effectively, and the power of mirror neurons in the brain. The tools are in the form of action steps that will allow you to become your authentic self.

Conditioning

As you will recall from Chapter 2, "conditioning" is the process of you metamorphosizing into who you needed to become to receive love from your caregivers at a very early age. Now, you get to decide who you want to be for yourself! If you are often angry or resentful of others, or if you struggle to communicate your needs or wants or to be present in your day-to-day life, this is for you! This course identifies your conditioning so you can heal your inner child, learn about the inner child archetypes and how to reparent yourself, identify your core values, and live with authenticity. The action steps will guide you through the process of further developing the beautiful you!

Befriend the Ego and Shadow Self

Here, you will learn about the ego, how the ego is developed, how your ego may keep you stuck in patterns of behavior that no longer serve you, the stories your ego may tell you, how the "shadow self" shows up in your life, and how to integrate the ego and shadow self. Release your ego's stories through this course!

More Cowbell

In this course, we discuss energy centers, vibrations, heart coherence, and the types of meditations that are most effective. We get spiritual!

The empowered freedom you will feel from understanding yourself better and embracing choice will be mindblowing. This course is my favorite.

I am certified to facilitate spiritual ceremonies and sound baths, so I am qualified to lead you down this path.

That's all, folks (as Porky Pig would say)! What you do with your journey from here is entirely up to you.

Let me ask you, which road will you take? Is it the road to your valor?

Two roads diverged in a yellow wood,
And sorry I could not travel both
And be one traveler, long I stood
And looked down one as far as I could
To where it bent in the undergrowth;

Then took the other, as just as fair,
And having perhaps the better claim,
Because it was grassy and wanted wear;
Though as for that the passing there
Had worn them really about the same,

And both that morning equally lay
In leaves no step had trodden black.
Oh, I kept the first for another day!
Yet knowing how way leads on to way,
I doubted if I should ever come back.

I shall be telling this with a sigh
Somewhere ages and ages hence:
Two roads diverged in a wood, and I –
I took the one less traveled by,
And that has made all the difference.

— *The Road Not Taken*, Robert Frost[10]

Taking the road less traveled has made all the difference in my life, and the same can happen for you.

While dissecting yourself can be a difficult task, you can count on me to put you back together at heart. Invest in yourself and step into your valor. It will impact the generations to come.

---

[10] Frost, R. (1915): *The Road Not Taken. The Atlantic Monthly.* Retrieved on November 28, 2024, from www.theatlantic.com/magazine/archive/1915/08/the-road-not-taken/645332

Acknowledgments

I have nothing but gratitude at the forefront of my mind for those that I've been honored to work with and to share my work with, whether it be this book, my courses, or my online community. It's been a privilege to grow and learn with each of you.

To those who have supported me and continue to remain by my side: my love for you is eternal. There have been so many whose impact on my growth has been huge. I can't possibly mention you all, but please know the gratitude I have for you will live on forever. Special mention goes to Kerrie Conrad, my BFF.

To my husband, Michael. Thank you for being my mirror and for having the courage it takes to grow together. Our love goes beyond the heathiest of loves we've ever known. You are without question the person who has held my heart, believed in me, and encouraged me to keep going and never give up the most. This endeavor would not have been possible without you. Words fail to express my gratitude, so I'll include a poem that I have written just for you:

Our love story is
Still my favorite
Ever told
Each other's heart
Forever we hold
Not to be bought
Certain to not be sold
The rhythm beats

On and on
And continues to unfold
In this life and the next
It is known
Embracing the bold
Open and running free
This love, this bliss
Truer than gold
For you, For me
Forever Yours, Denise

To my counselor, Ron Deluca, who told me it wasn't my fault and that I was a good person when I needed it most. I'm extremely grateful for that and for you planting the original seed of me writing my story. I could not have begun this journey without you.

To my mentor, Heather. You are my Ambassador of Quan. Without you, my healing and spiritual journey home would've been nonexistent. Thank you for opening my eyes to the true beauty that lies within us all.

To my daughters, Grace and Maggie. You are my "why." You are the reason I have fought as hard as I have to heal, break generational trauma in our family lineage, and help other parents on their journey. While I'm not perfect and have made many mistakes, I want you to know that you are a gift to this world and my heart. I am forever grateful that you were brought into my life. "She believed she could, so she did."

To my publisher, Hayley Paige at Onyx Publishing, who I instantly resonated with and knew my story was in the right hands with. I am forever grateful for your guidance, kindness, and authenticity.

To Faye, my editor, who not only saw my vision, but wholeheartedly helped bring it to light and worked tirelessly with me for two years throughout the writing and editing process. So grateful for you.

To the team at Onyx Publishing that worked on the beautiful cover and for your guidance throughout the entire process: I am forever indebted to you. My heart is full of love and gratitude for each of you.

And to my readers: as you continue on your journey, know that with every end comes a new beginning, and that I'm grateful for you. My hope is that you will pass this book along and share it with the collective, creating a better world for all.

About the Author

Denise Conde has spent her lifetime being in service to others. She retired after twenty years as an educator, has a master's degree in education, is trained in trauma informed care, and is the co-owner of Conde Design Group, LLC (which specializes in custom kitchen cabinetry and interior millwork). She is also a certified sacred ceremonies facilitator, sound healer, and peer mentor to Gen Xers on their healing journey.

Denise Conde is constantly expanding her reach through her daily content online (@your.valor), and has several courses at www.deniseconde.com dedicated to guiding Gen Xers through the journey of stepping into their valor.

Denise lives in her hometown of Youngstown, NY.

www.ingramcontent.com/pod-product-compliance
Lightning Source LLC
Chambersburg PA
CBHW031434270326
41930CB00007B/696